THE STORY OF ADA:
A SPIRITUAL JOURNEY
THROUGH DREAMS

From Awareness to Self-Discovery

MAVIS ALDRIDGE, PHD

BALBOA
PRESS

A DIVISION OF HAY HOUSE

Balboa Press books may be ordered through booksellers or by contacting:

Balboa Press
A Division of Hay House
1663 Liberty Drive
Bloomington, IN 47403
www.balboapress.com
1 (877) 407-4847

Because of the dynamic nature of the Internet, any web addresses or links contained in this book may have changed since publication and may no longer be valid. The views expressed in this work are solely those of the author and do not necessarily reflect the views of the publisher, and the publisher hereby disclaims any responsibility for them.

The author of this book does not dispense medical advice or prescribe the use of any technique as a form of treatment for physical, emotional, or medical problems without the advice of a physician, either directly or indirectly. The intent of the author is only to offer information of a general nature to help you in your quest for emotional and spiritual well-being. In the event you use any of the information in this book for yourself, which is your constitutional right, the author and the publisher assume no responsibility for your actions.

Any people depicted in stock imagery provided by Thinkstock are models, and such images are being used for illustrative purposes only.
Certain stock imagery © Thinkstock.

Printed in the United States of America.

ISBN: 978-1-4525-1760-5 (sc)
ISBN: 978-1-4525-1761-2 (e)

Balboa Press rev. date: 08/01/2014

I dedicate this book:

To my dear mother, Beatrice, who inspired me in my childhood to appreciate dreams as channels of information bringing messages from my soul.

To my brothers and sisters who also dream and share their dreams with passion.

To all the dream teachers whose writings and teachings have helped me to recognize the relationship between my dreams and my spiritual growth.

To all dreamers at this time of cosmic change, whose dreams are leading them to the discovery of themselves, their uniqueness, and the gift of their lives.

To the Forces in the Universe, which, despite my blindness, have continued to embrace, love, and compassionately guide me along my continuing inner journey.

Acknowledgements

I wish to thank Lillian, my former professor, whose tutelage for a dissertation facilitated the understanding of the language of dreams; Connie's valuable insights were gratefully received and enriched my original perspective of my dreams through the universal principles she described. Carolyn's encouraging comments provided a needed boost at a time when the continuation of writing was at a critical and tedious stage. I extend a special gratitude to the Universe through my interactions with Nature as my constant teacher, and all the lessons from personal encounters without which my life would not have revealed the meaning of its journey with such perfection.

I would like to express my deep gratitude to Staci, Maneli and the Design Team at Balboa Press.

CONTENTS

INTRODUCTION

One day, Ada and her friend Rose met at the Barnes and Noble Bookstore at Sumter Landing in Florida, where they planned to have coffee and enjoy each other's company once again. Ada was always delighted to see her busy friend, if for nothing else, it would be to learn about her new plans and projects. When she arrived, Ada was already delving in her dream journal, reading some of the entries which dated back to the eighties. As Rose, smiling, always fashionably dressed, seated herself in the opposite chair, Ada asked, "Would you like to hear some of my dreams?" "Sure," she immediately replied. Ada warned her that after hearing them she may think Ada is a prime candidate for the straight jacket. Rose gazed at Ada with a look that registered, "Why don't you try me?"

Ada read a few of her dreams to her dear friend, looking up after each one to see if her facial expression had changed. After reading the tenth dream entry, Ada looked at her surprisingly. Rose responded with a question that sent Ada into spasms of laughter. "Why do you dream so much?" she demanded to know. "I haven't got the faintest idea," Ada retorted, "am I supposed to be responsible for them?" "Do you sleep at night at all?" Rose blurted with much consternation on her face. "Of course," Ada responded, "that's when all this drama goes on! But you know, Rose, you asked a very, very important question that I have never considered. Yes, it is important to know why I dream so much!"

Until then, the meaning of Ada's dreams wavered between mystery, curiosity, delight, flights of fancy, and wonder about her sanity. For the most part, they were just variegated nocturnal adventures, some perhaps as rehearsals of daytime dramas, but all in all, nothing to be concerned about. Now the *WHY* of Rose's question, a concept that was never an issue, became the springboard for a new found curiosity, the focus for a challenging exploration into Ada's subconscious that she was ill-prepared to undertake. Yet, the challenge beckoned her to take on the audacity of a daring archaeologist preparing for an uncertain dig, hoping that buried clues will eventually emerge to provide some answers.

Ada began feeling like an archaeologist which Sarah Breathnach identifies as one who uses physical or documentary evidence for a dig. Ada's documentary evidence involved three volumes of dreams, recordings and related comments which began graphically in the 1980's, but in memory from Ada's teen years! "*Why* so many dreams with such frequency, often three in the same night?" she began asking herself. "*Why* am I targeted to have them? *Why* do they continue when some of my friends say they don't even dream at all? What is their purpose? *Why* are they wrapped in metaphorical language often so baffling to decipher leaving her thinking they are just passing neurological processes of the brain during the night?" she ranted mentally. Ada realized that in order to answer the *Why* questions, the *What* and *When* must be examined from the earliest dream years, to the current period of her advanced senior years.

She decided with much trepidation to undertake the dig, trusting that the same Source that infiltrated her subconscious with dreams will also guide the exploration, provide the clues, the finds, the messages, possible lessons, and finally revealing the *WHY*!! *The Story of Ada* reveals events in Ada's life, and dreams which predicted them, most of which she understood much later. In addition are her deep inner musings, experiences, and reflections which embrace the broader spectrum of life's events illuminating her adventure towards self-understanding. Her unique quest can inspire others to enrich their lives by exploring the secret, seemingly abandoned corridors of the subconscious, along their own spiritual, evolutionary journey to authentic self-discovery.

Ada will be her own relentless heroine on the journey, excavating memories, battling doubts, conquering challenges, reliving emotional wounds and setbacks, perhaps occasionally feeling healed, all in pursuit of an intangible, elusive, but perhaps accessible treasure to be identified within herself. Despite the possible defeats Ada anticipated in the process of this dig, she promised herself to remain indomitable. Perhaps, at times she will even pretend bravery, feel victorious, and hopefully, in the end, to be experientially transformed and gratified as a heroine on her own retrospective and introspective spiritual journey through her dreams. The quest became a daunting, yet compelling endeavor.

CHAPTER ONE

...life is a sacred adventure of the soul. Our souls have inner yearnings and mystical secrets ready for our discovery when we pay attention to our lives and to our dreams... Our dreams and visions become guideposts along the way. Barrick[1].

Those of us who take this spiritual journey seriously devote time and energy to deepen and evolve our knowledge of it. We study how the masters and mystics have taken the journey and we strive to be conscious of our own spiritual unfolding. Kaplan[2].

HOW IT ALL BEGAN

A Mom's Influence

As a child, Ada often heard her mother, Beatrice, speak about dreams she had the night before. She expressed them as though they were a sacred experience and was even able to interpret their meaning in relation to a current situation or a pending event. Ada was quietly impressed with her Mom's confidence. Although she often had doubts about the accuracy of the interpretations, Ada was convinced that Bea intuitively knew she was her own seasoned guru when it came to understanding her dreams. For example, when Ada's brother, Vin had a tractor accident which ended in a court case and his companion was fatally injured, Mom dreamed that she saw angels dancing around a fire, and as a result, she knew that the case would end in Vin's favor, and so it did. When Ada sat for a difficult examination in her elementary school years, doubting that she would be successful, Mom assured her, "Don't worry, you are going to pass! Last night I had a dream that somebody gave me a glass of milk and I drank every bit!" Again, without objecting to the seeming mismatch of dream elements and the reality of the events, young Ada wondered how Mom could be so sure she was right. Yet, "dancing angels" "fire" and "glass of milk" were images written indelibly in Ada's memory, images Mom associated with good news, images that would much later be among symbolic events in Ada's own prolific dream life!

It was as though Bea had a special intuitive gift, a legacy of dreaming, which it seems by association, she would pass on to Ada and some of her siblings, although in a much limited version. As for her Dad, Mom's dreams and the meanings she assigned to them were not only abnormal, they were downright irrational, far-fetched, and definitely superstitious. However, the impact on Ada was formidable, and continued to be so even now in her late senior years when she no more has doubts of the significance of her dreams.

Early Awareness of Her Dreams

Ada remembers her first dream very vividly. She was born in Jamaica, and at about age fifteen, she had taken the Third Jamaica Local, another of those difficult essay type examinations which consisted of eight subjects based on the English system. Failing one subject meant taking all eight again after preparing for another whole year. It was a rigorous experience she dreaded so she studied much more than was necessary in order to avoid the repetition. Of course, she became anxious about the results. Shortly before they were published, she dreamed of a huge bird's nest with colorful birds playfully flying in and out of it. She enjoyed the dream because birds had been her favorite creatures. Their instinct for survival, unique characteristics, their wide variety, their ability to soar with spontaneity and freedom, and cover long distances with such small bodies filled her with admiration. "What myriad exotic places they must see," Ada often pondered with slight envy. With glee, thanksgiving, and relief she received the news that she was among the successful candidates that year. Did she associate her dream of birds with her success? Not then, but birds was just the beginning of a long list in her later dream repertoire of nature symbols close to her heart, including rivers, oceans, waterfalls, fountains, animals, flowers, fruits, and all the vibrant colors associated with them.

For many years, Ada held the belief that dreams with such symbols were only reflecting her love of nature which had become a vehicle for stimulation and personal, private joy. She could recall times in her childhood when Mom recruited her as bearer of gifts and messages for her uncle who lived far up in the hills of Mount Pleasant. Ada's private thrill was to leave early in the morning, sit on a rock near a clump of trees near her uncle's house where she not only caught the whiffs of ripening spice pimento, but she had the exciting privilege of being shrouded in the enchanting morning mist. She could delightfully greet the magically spreading silver shafts of sunlight just as they were peeping over the horizon. After some tantalizing moments of increasing brightness and dancing color flares, the rays would suddenly burst into a radiant glittering golden ball amid wispy white clouds and a light blue sky. After she had her thrill and fill of her private fun show, so divinely directed, she left as if walking on air to complete the errand for Mom. Ada recalled on one occasion, after greeting her uncle, he stood silently for a few moments, skeptically gazing at her as if she were a rare specimen from Mars.

Other fascinations were part of her inventory of secret delights. Ada loved to stand under the arch formed by the trees over the roadway at a special area half-way on the hill on the six-mile journey from school. With her classmates some distance ahead, for her, that area became enchanted during dark winter evenings, as the arching tree branches cast their magical spell of artistic patterns on the road in the bright moon light. Except for the out-of-space sounds from the orchestra of night insects and the owl, or the intermittent glitter of fireflies, there was a soothing silence tempting her to lie right there and go to sleep over the lace-patterned shadows in the middle of the road. It was a heavenly experience under the canopy of branches penetrated by beckoning rays of bright stars and the all-embracing light of the moon.

Following her transported session, she hurried to rejoin the group of boys and girls still engaged in their own world of taunts, raucous laughter, and wild, uninteresting chatter which sounded as if no one was listening to anyone, yet everyone seemed to be enjoying everyone else's company. They had no idea of the fantastic excursion Ada had just experienced. Was she missed? Perhaps they were accustomed to Ada's "oddities" and she felt glad that no one ever asked as to her whereabouts as she would have been stumped to explain!

For a long time, it was her belief that dreams of stars, moonlight, trees, sunlight, and hill climbs were just modified reenactments of her childhood's intimate connections with nature rightfully earning inclusion in her dream symbols inventory. However, one day, in a casual conversation and sharing, another special friend, also astounded at some of her dreams, commented, "Ada, you have not yet begun to understand the meanings of your dreams!" In that moment, her friend's observation sounded trivial and meaningless, but later, when Ada began exploring her records of forgotten dreams, she realized how absolutely and profoundly correct her friend was. Now, after three decades and three volumes of entries with comments on coinciding events, Ada arrived at a point of acute awareness that her dreams have been reflections of a fascinating spiritual journey which she began feeling compelled to explore. Psychologically, believe it or not, it was a heroine's daunting journey!

CHAPTER TWO

"...To deny a dream is to deny a part of ourselves. Dreams are an instant connection to our unconscious. It is a place of mystery and the unknown...A moderate attempt to interpret our dreams will lead to greater self-understanding and awareness, as well as to moments of enlightenment resulting in greater consciousness." (*www.dreamtalk.htm,.p.1*[1]

Something More is that mysterious, missing, odd-fitting piece of ourselves, and Spirit is determined we're going to find it one way or another... Breathnach,[2]

A RECURRING DREAM
AND A FLOWER SPEAKS

Following graduation from a Catholic Teacher's College Ada delved into teaching in Catholic Schools for several years with unstinting dedication. This was nurtured by her early association with clergy, and nuns with whom she lived and worked for several decades, beginning in her teen years. It was a long, mysterious connection which Ada will always hold with deep reverence. But that is another intricate story to be told. How does one explain an irresistible compulsion which led to a series of intriguing experiences comparable to the beginning and end of a long chapter, complete in itself, yet related to the other sections in a mystery book? In general, Ada enjoyed the opportunities for creative expression in her overall teaching career which spanned kindergarten, elementary, secondary, and college levels. During the period of one administrative assignment in a secondary school while in Jamaica, she had a recurring dream.

> *I am climbing a rock with very sharp edges; I am making no progress and my hands and knees are bruised and bleeding.*

Even after the third occurrence, Ada remained unaware of the message of this dream. She made no connection with the circumstances of her daily life. It was just another dream, although so different from the presence of birds. By that time Ada was more mature, deeply involved with school activities, enjoying the challenges and demands of working with parents and students, organizing meetings, garden parties, regional science fairs, and graduation exercises. She felt" fulfilled," always aspiring to new endeavors, never experiencing a dull moment, as there was always another goal yet to be accomplished, another event for which to plan and prepare.

Despite her apparent "successes," there was a nagging sense of emptiness, of something missing, an awareness, a hunger, a beckoning towards an unidentifiable, elusive reach. Since climbing a rock, bleeding and getting nowhere on the climb did not stir her curiosity enough about the message from the dream, something else more tangible and striking would, in time, arrest her attention.

She regularly passed and admired the flowers in the garden near the St. Joseph's building every morning on the way to the school office. One particular morning, the bed of pink and white begonia blossoms seemed much more alive and colorful than ever before. As a matter of fact, the blossoms were so abundant that the stems bent with the weight of the rich clusters as if to command attention. It seemed even the leaves became fewer in order to accommodate the volume of the blooms. Thoughts of the Creator filled Ada's mind; she stopped in her tracks as this was such an unusual sight to behold! It was as though she were looking at them through new lens, and without knowing the full meaning of her words, or how she was prompted to say them, she uttered a self-affirming statement, "This is how I am meant to be...*BLOOMING!* It was a pivotal moment, but what did it mean? Ada was getting a message, not from a book, a mentor, or sermon, but from something whispered to her from that which was non-human, voiceless, and concrete! Without any clarity about how her "blooming" could occur or how it would unfold, she knew without the slightest doubt that her time in that "fulfilling" administrative position had ended.

Shortly after, with the help of several angels in disguise, acting at various junctures of time, the mechanisms for entry to the United Sates were set in motion and executed. An interesting set of circumstances led her to the huge, cosmopolitan city of New York where she finally landed. Beginning in January

1976, her life underwent dramatic changes during which dreaming and her forgotten desire to be blooming became inextricably intertwined. Only after many years, the *What* and the *When* would provide the constructs to determine the Why of her intended mysterious dream journey, a journey which can only be undertaken with determination to find clues with the strategies of an archaeologist and the relentless courage of a heroine.

CHAPTER THREE

To the disbelieving, dreams may simply be a puzzling, disturbing or totally irrelevant phenomenon. To the individual who desires self-improvement and communication with his divine self, dreams will show the way. To the dedicated person who seeks to serve his fellowmen and God, dreams will bring understanding, joy, and peace of mind, for they are the magic mirror of the soul. Sechrist[1]

A DOOR OPENS AND A
NEW LIFE BEGINS

With a total of three hundred dollars in her pocket, and without knowing how it would happen, Ada originally planned to stay only two years the most in New York City to earn a Master's Degree. The spectacle of winter boots, coat and gloves was intimidating. The thought of her gnashing teeth in the cold season strengthened her resolve but apparently the Universe had other plans for the blooming, whatever that meant. It turned out that six years of academic studies including three years of college teaching had passed when she suffered an agonizing experience in 1982. Both her parents passed away, three months apart.

Ada was devastated, and her siblings by then were scattered far and wide in distant areas. In order to reconnect, all agreed to a reunion in Jamaica within a specified period. Before the reunion Ada had this dream:

> *There are two spaceships with circular rims moving in the sky. The rims are beautiful with bright, colored lights and long rays of white lights trailing behind them. One spaceship is flying ahead of the other.*

This dream, still indelibly imprinted in her memory, needed no recording on paper and seemingly had no immediate relevance to Ada's current activities. In retrospect, the dream meant that her siblings would first arrive for the reunion as planned; Ada would be the spaceship behind because she would be detained after realizing that her work visa had expired and she would be delayed one week for it to be renewed. The colored lights indicated the joys to be felt, and the circular rims, the promise of a reunion fulfilled.

Another remarkable dream came to Ada shortly after her mother's passing. She originally interpreted it to mean that Mom was happy and contented in her new abode and Ada should be comforted. As recommended in a dream course given by Jeremy Taylor, author of *Where People Fly and Water Runs Uphill,* all the dreams in this book are written in present tense as if reliving the experience.

> ***Mom is sitting sideways on a white horse. She is smiling as usual and looks regal, dressed in a long, satin, purple gown. At the front of the gown is a separate panel in the skirt draped in folds and clasped on her left hip with a circular brooch set with glistening colored stones. She wears a headdress, a turban, plaited at the sides and clasped in the middle of her forehead with a smaller version of the brooch on her hips. Around her neck is a circular, many stranded necklace, also with shining stones.***

After waking from this indelible dream, Ada thought to herself, "Thanks Mom for the visit! You are in a place of happiness and peace! I am glad. You are beautiful!" The dream endorsed Dr. Thurston's view, based on Cayce's teachings, that genuine communication has been made when a dream of a departed love one conveys assurances of love and life beyond the grave.

Later, in a chance encounter with a well-known clairvoyant, Ada was informed that her Mom was indeed happy and that she was communicating with Ada from Egypt, a place where she had spent several lifetimes. Indicated by Mom's garb and jewelry, the explanation sounded plausible and gave Ada the impression that there was a strong, unique connection between her and her mother which she was not yet quite conscious of, but would realize later.

In her grieving moments Ada wondered how she could ever permanently return home without seeing her parents, loving them, and receiving their love, hugging them as she often did before. She was unable to tell her Dad that she had finished that "long essay" he was eager for her to complete so that she could return home. But in an uncanny way, their parting provided the deciding factor, that is, their tacit permission for staying in The Big Apple, the environment which would eventually provide a new trajectory for her life. It seemed destined to be the place where dreams would play a major role in her life's unfolding through the people, places, and circumstances that the universe had pre-arranged, thus leading her gradually to awareness and self-understanding of her slowly emerging, new self.

After several years, the task of exploring her dreams would become a baffling spiritual archaeological inner journey, an experience for grasping the *What* and the *When,* leading hopefully to definitively reveal the *Why.*

CHAPTER FOUR

Dreamwork provides a viable route to claiming our higher qualities and getting acquainted with the person we are meant to become. In so doing we gradually transform ourselves and enrich our lives and the lives of those around us. Barrick,[1].

Truly, they are an art form of the soul for creative self-expression, self-discovery, and self-healing. Webb[2].

As you unfold the meaning of your dream messages, you discover the mysterious process of self-revelation. It's an exciting journey. Barrick[3].

THE BEGINNING OF PROFOUND CHANGES

In 1988, Ada began a journal for no special purpose except to record special day occurrences and a few night happenings from her subconscious! She could not foresee in the next decade and after, that her dreams would continue in a strange and wonderful profusion to be understood to some degree several years later in her retirement years.

Did she dream in the six years after her parents' passing in 1982? Most likely, but perhaps the pressure of still adjusting to a new cultural and professional environment, finally settling to a full time position, and learning the mechanisms for survival, most likely suppressed the memory of them. They must have blinded her to any relevance or any instructional significance they might have had.

It is very tempting at this point to begin to list some of Ada's outstanding dreams beginning in 1988, however, it is necessary to first provide the reader with a backdrop from which to view them. This much can be said, that many times after waking from her dreams, she was filled with elation as well as consternation. That was all. The pervading belief of understanding their frequency and meaning, was that they were, for the most part, modified replays of her avid love of nature, children, or her walking meditation experiences. They were all, in essence, just mind-over-matter reenacted scenarios. However, years later, much to her chagrin, her conclusions proved not entirely wrong, but extremely superficial. Her dreams held tantalizing secrets to a self that would take time on a long journey of changes for her to wake up and discover the jewels within them!

CHAPTER FIVE

On the way to authenticity, on the way to our soul-driven need to discover Something More...we must pass through the Valley of the Shadow of Discouragement, Denial, Doubt, and Darkness before we emerge into the Light of Something More. Breathnach[1]

...don't try and play someone else's role; play your own...knowing yourself is the source of change for your life. We change our reality by changing what is within us. This is our place of wholeness. Praagh[2]

EMPTINESS AGAIN
REARS ITS HEAD

During the eventful decade 1988 to 1998, Ada became much more active, and at the time she hardly recognized the breadth of her involvement in academic activities and extra-curricular pursuits. In this context, it was as if she were being driven along by a current of favorable ideas and circumstances. However, as broadening as those activities proved to be, including meeting and sharing with cooperative, hard-working new colleagues, she remembered experiencing at various intervals, that familiar, uncanny sense of emptiness and restlessness again! She tried to be more fervent in prayer and meditation, always questioning why this feeling had returned when she thought she had been trying so hard to "toe the line" in her spiritual and temporal endeavors. Again, as in her pre-New York years, she was caught up in the world of being active, achieving goals, and the pursuit of "success."

"Have I not studied hard enough in six years?" Ada frustratingly questioned herself. "Haven't I been generously conducting choirs, and regularly planning liturgy and playing the organ at church services, singing and playing at funerals, continuing to be a devoted Catholic, even volunteering at a homeless shelter, visiting the sick and homebound? How much more diligent could I be in teaching, attending, organizing, chairing conferences, as well as presenting at workshops locally and internationally? Colleagues of good-will have valued my work and endorsed my bid for promotions. Haven't I been" blooming?" "Aren't my blooms enough?" she continued ranting with frustrating and increased emotional vehemence. " What more could be required of me? Shouldn't I be more happy now?

Must all the feelings of contentment I have had be mere transitory experiences? Isn't this the reach that was previously outside my grasp that I felt from the begonia blossoms, years earlier? Is there a ghost following me? If I were given a million dollars or won the lottery, this sense of hunger for "something more" would still have remained unsatisfied. What is it within me that I long for but cannot identify? Is there something else that I am supposed to have but may never have? Will I even recognize it if it happened? I ask again, is there a ghost following me? Is there a relationship between my dreams and this emptiness? Why! Why! Why! Is the universe with me or not? God, are you out there?" Ada asked the empty air fiercely, and received emptiness and a terrifying silence in return. Great, she might as well had stoned the wind.

She was becoming angry, scared, frustrated, and frighteningly alone! She wondered, "Is this what Francis Thompson felt when he wrote the *Hound of Heaven?* Is it *The Dark Night of the Soul* experienced by St. John of the Cross, or the "desert period" often mentioned by some spiritual seekers?" Ada was sure she was not even near their category, but became aware of the veracity of Kaplan's description of the spiritual journey as "a difficult climb" and Sylvia Browne's reference to it as comparable" to birth pains!" That's encouraging, Ada thought.

Ada realized that her educated, restless self was far from providing her the happiness or the blooming she had anticipated. She began feeling as though in addition to her "regular" self, she had two other selves, a professional and a spiritual self, each struggling for dominance over the other. Perhaps a break could give some clarity, she thought, but how would any such understanding even occur? Wouldn't that be just a change of pace and place? Perhaps she should take a sabbatical in the Fall; that could at least bring some relaxation, a small measure of healing, and stillness to her fevered, frustrated, confused mind, as well as balance to her exhausted body and restless spirit. A rested mind can better provide clarity of thought.

After confiding her plight to her close and very dear friend Monsy, she responded with much sincerity, "Ada, if you had a husband and a few children, you would not feel that way. Ada, I always wondered when you would get married. And I believe you would make a wonderful wife and mother! Don't get me wrong, I just want the best for you!" After expressing thanks to Monsy, Ada, conscious of her inner dilemma of not knowing and trying desperately to understand herself, realized that following that counsel was tantamount to making a deliberate choice to enter The Valley of Decline and No Return.

Intuitively, Ada was certain from very early in her life that she did not want to be a mother, a nurse, or a secretary! Even now in her senior years, she is certain that none of those choices would have served her well on her path to self-discovery in this life! Now, into the dig after several decades, Ada's decisions for her life were further confirmed by Praagh who warns not to play someone else's role, and states that knowing oneself is the source of change which leads to wholeness. Breathnach also advises to live by one's own lights and not the opinion of others. While certain assets are valuable, she adds an enlightening eye-opener, "Money, marital status, fame, admiration, and accomplishment mean nothing if the soul is starving."[3]. There was definitely no mistake, Ada's soul was starving for "something more" despite all her previous spiritual devotions of frequent attendance at Mass, Novenas, Rosaries, good deeds, and educational accomplishments!

Some Solace and Serenity

Ada frequently uttered gratitude to the Creator for Central Park, her second home, playground, and secret enchanted garden. There she could enjoy a variety of thrilling distractions from flowers and butterflies to turtles and squirrels, changing colors of the seasons to nude trees in winter, spellbinding orchestral music on the Great Lawn to Shakespearian drama at the Delacorte Theatre, ethnic music and dancing, to a walk or jog around the reservoir, as well as visits to the museums of Art and Natural History. In the park, alone, or meeting with friends or family, Ada found some temporary solace and uplifting serenity. Yet, that was what it was, temporary. The yearning persisted, and there was no escaping. She remained stupefied at her night adventures, and became progressively more serious and faithful in recording them as if she were zealously expecting a drama to be played out. Sometimes it felt similar to the occasion when she separated from the children on the road during her elementary school days, totally oblivious of what she was truly experiencing. The dreams sometimes felt like a trip to a distant, yet immediate nowhere space, thrilling, magical, and tantalizing. Ada realized that there are some things that are deeply felt beyond words, too profound to be immediately understood, a reality that escapes explanation, at least for some time.

CHAPTER SIX

"...we sense that something is missing in our lives and fruitlessly search 'out there' for the answers...what's often wrong is that we are disconnected from an authentic sense of self." Breathnach[1]

When we take time and devote ourselves to exploring who we truly are, we will open to the various levels of consciousness. We will soon find we are much more than our physical appearance and physical lives, for the physical is merely the tip of the iceberg. Praagh[2].

A SABBATICAL YEAR
AND A SHIFT

In the Fall of 1990, after eleven years of hard work and major emotional and physical adjustments in a new metropolitan city, Ada was able to relax during a sabbatical, and she often beseeched the universe to generously bless all whom she encountered since her entry into New York City to make her experiences possible, and wished for them lives flowing with joyful abundance. Any attempt to express the rich, spiritual nourishment she gained from the gift of a sabbatical year would be limited, but it was a turning point with results which she could never have imagined!

Dreams in the Yucatan

Like so many mysterious events in her life, it is impossible for Ada to explain why she chose Merida in the Yucatan Peninsula where she spent a month during her sabbatical year in 1990. She had a sudden interest in Mayan culture which became so compelling that she visited several temples including the renowned Pyramid of Kukulcan at Chicken Itza, an edifice of architectural and symbolic genius of the ancients. Little did she know that this place she visited so long ago was the beginning of a cyclic personal experience, and would in 2012 become a magnetic hub of activity for a global spiritual community. For Ada, learning about the Mayans turned out to be the sacred portal or entry point for visits to a whole host of other awesome sites in other mysterious energy centers of the world including Egypt, Greece, Stonehenge, Glastonbury, and Macchu Pichu. The visits to the temples in Merida seemed also to have initiated her into other several dream experiences during her sabbatical, some of which are grouped below in a series, and listed in three phases.

In the Fall of 1990, Ada recorded the following dreams she had in Merida, a city in the Yucatan peninsula in Mexico.

Dreams during the Sabbatical Year –
The Early Phase – SERIES A

- *I am standing in an elevated area where everything is in beautiful pink and white colors. I am amazed, so there I stand calling everyone to come and look!*
- *I take an examination. I must answer some questions on a test. The presider is pleased with the answers, and he says, "O.K. Quite good!"*
- *To get to a church, I must walk up a steep slope at the top of which is a hole. I put my hand in it, and someone from inside grasps my hand to help me to the top.!*
- *There is a healthy plant growing out of a wall and as I look at it, it extends a branch with flower buds already opening to bloom. I call a man standing nearby to come and see the unusual spectacle!*

At first glance, although Ada enjoyed them, none of these dreams bore any association to any of her activities while in Merida. Other than meeting new friends and visiting the historic sites, she saw many flowers, she took no examinations and the church she attended was not located at the top of a slope! Before daybreak on her last sleepless night in Merida, she spent an hour walking along the high green hedges of the neighborhood in the fresh, cool, misty morning air perfumed with the fragrance of gardenia blossoms. But to what should she connect those dreams?

CHAPTER SEVEN

Personal dreaming is a stage in which we are asked to broaden personal belief systems and to mature spiritually...ask us to grow to open our minds, to open those letters...to expand one's belief system so deeper truths can be accessed. Kaplan[1].

Once you are aware that life is about flow, that our energy fields are constantly overlapping...you'll have a fuller openness to synchronicities, a form of grace...these "inspired coincidences" are moments of perfect timing when things fall into place with startling precision. Orloff[2]

ANSWERS FROM AN UNEXPECTED SOURCE

Angelic messengers are truly around us in human form. Ada had learned that many times, and they make contact to give us information when we are ready to receive them. Another related saying of a Sufi teacher states, "when the student is ready, the teacher appears." She must have been ready, because one such messenger with whom she spent much time in Merida, was Sarah, a Canadian, who initiated a greeting at a party. She invited Ada to her home where they conversed on spiritual topics as though they had known each other for decades. Through this encounter, Ada was enlightened and lifted out of herself. Late in the evening of their day together, a special moment came when Sarah reached for one of her precious books on reincarnation from her library, lovingly presented it to Ada while emphatically requesting its return. As it was near Ada's time for departure from Merida, she read it all through the night in order to return it the next day. Ada did not know it then, but when Sarah introduced her to the works of Paramahansa Yogananda, Ruth Montgomery, and Edgar Cayce's philosophy on dreams and reincarnation, she became hooked for life on spiritual food which would nourish her for the rest of her life. In that cool morning air shortly before her departure, walking and inhaling the perfume of the gardenia blossoms, Ada felt a newness within her, peaceful, uplifting, exhilarating. But, again, how in the name of sanity, did the dreams fit into all this?

Mavis Aldridge, PhD

Interpretations of Dreams in the Yucatan

Only now in her mature years is Ada able to unravel some of the *what* linked with the *when* of those dreams. The list of four dreams above could be represented in a story about her. It seems the experience in Merida placed her in an elevated aspect of herself and of joyful change represented by the raised area in pink and white colors. By calling and inviting someone to come and see something unusual, Ada was expressing her fascination and willingness to accept and share the new knowledge expressed to her through Sarah. She found the new teachings on reincarnation mind-expanding, refreshing and mysterious, yet logical. In the process of reaching a raised level in her spiritual growth symbolized by the church, she must undertake the challenge of a "steep slope," a difficult uphill spiritual journey. However, "someone inside grasps my hand" seems to indicate that guidance along the way, such as Sarah, would assist her in the climb. She must have been the plant growing out of a previously spiritually sterile environment, the wall, a former obstacle, a hardness and rigidity of thinking in her previous religious beliefs; she was now being rejuvenated, thriving, and growing taller.

CHAPTER EIGHT

If the false self keeps the personality operating at a diminished capacity, spiritual growth is virtually impossible. Being human becomes an experience of being broken, sinful, and hopeless. These are the lies of the false self. Kaplan[1]

Above all, they want to discover their more positive and authentic self which is hidden within. They pursue the understanding of their dreams as an avenue to an in-depth understanding of their soul and spirit. Barrick[2]

A STRANGER TO HERSELF

Back in New York after a month, Ada felt as if she had spent some time on another planet. Grateful that she was sane, sober, and still in her sabbatical year, she wasted no time delving into the many books Sarah had recommended. She spent many nights reading into the wee hours of the morning becoming familiar with the astounding writings of Yogananda and Montgomery whose many books still remain sacrosanct additions to her library. What many fascinating spiritual truths were being revealed! She did indeed feel like a growing plant! When Ada read the books of Edgar Cayce, especially some of the 14,000 readings he gave others based on his accurate trance connections with the Akashic Records, she was astounded and convinced that her inner archaeological heroic dig was already underway and proving rewarding although she was barely skimming the surface. She felt like one of the hungry waifs at a bakery window salivating over ideas of eastern Indian and Chinese philosophers, Zen Buddhism and Hindu religions, as well as about Cayce's phenomenal work in the U.S. She kept reminding herself of the importance of Cayce's recommendation, "Study self, study self." Isn't this similar to the message, "Know Thyself," written over the doorway of the Greek Temple at Delphi in Greece?

What became a solid topic of interest for Ada was reincarnation, defined by Cayce in reference to the soul, as "a way of growing back towards the divine; to perfect its attunement to the divine, and its loving service to its fellows."[3] When Cayce gave a reading, it was with reference to those two processes in the individual's current lifetime. Who was she before this lifetime, Ada began to wonder. Is her previous lifetime affecting her current one? Increasingly, she began to realize that there was something quite profound to her dreams, but it seemed she was yet too spiritually inept to grasp their full meaning, purpose, or their *Why*! She became impatient, yet she recognized the need to be patient. Unearthing evidence in an archaeological exploration takes time, attention to detail, alertness for clues, and above all, what Ada was short of, patience!

In her explorations, one text which proved particularly enlightening was Dr. Harmon Bro's *Edgar Cayce on Dreams,* the book that not only made Ada realize that she was part of a very large population of other dreamers who were not only sane and normal, they were also being sent sensitive messages from their subconscious through their dreams. Again, it has been said that when the student is ready, the teacher will appear; Ada, although somewhat scared, was ready for any source of enlightenment, and Cayce would become one of her foremost dream teachers who would help in understanding her dreams. Others would include remarkable trailblazers including Connie Kaplan, Elsie Sechrist, Sylvia Browne, Judith Orloff, and Marilyn Barrick.

At this stage in the dig, it was possible for Ada to look back with new found interest and curiosity, and examine more closely, the first set of her interesting, yet then obscure and puzzling dreams which occurred in the first half of 1990 long preceding her jolting sabbatical experiences in Merida. Now, their significance, in retrospect, became so much more illuminating.

Ada's Pre-Sabbatical Dreams – SERIES B

- *There is an orchard with colorful oranges and grapefruits; very large, ripe, inviting, and ready to eat.*
- *In a play ready to be staged, I forget my lines; when I get the script from someone, there is no play.*

- ***While standing, I am looking at a badly shattered mirror.***
- ***In a cleared area, I begin walking and then develop high speed running. People watch amazed as I pass by as if I am an athlete.***
- ***I enter an unusual house with several sections. One room is decorated with beautiful Chinese tapestry. In another are worn shoes, and among them a pair of green leather walking shoes. They seem oversize at first, but when I try on the first one, I could not get my heel into it!***
- ***Another fruit tree has several huge, large, colorful, ripe, round oranges.***
- ***Two beautiful exotic birds stand before me. Such birds I have never seen before and I am in awe of their rich, bright colors.***
- ***It is a clear blue night sky, and one particular star is very bright.***
- ***I am in the company of Chinese youth. (Two nights in a row).***

Ada was certainly intrigued on reading Cayce's statement that dreams occur to provide an experience, that the *dreamer is central* to the information, that there is *a purpose*, and *change* is their intention! Similar to the dreams in Mexico, as the dreamer, Ada thought she was central to a story of the meanings of the above dreams, but her grasp of their purpose was superficial at best. She was already experiencing change, indeed, a strange inner change in which she still felt alone, yet, quite oddly, never lonely. Is there more change to come? She realized she was having a separate existence in exploring strange territory! She wondered what it would be like, aware that it may still be beyond words or only a superficial grasp.

In the above dreams, "forgetting my lines" in a play, which suggested lack of preparation or readiness, the only association she could make was a disappointment she had with a search for a house during that period. Engaging in that search was a financial loss and an ill-timed transaction. The end result was no house, as in "no play" after being shown a few houses by agents. On the other hand, another meaning could be that Ada was ill-prepared for the challenges that lay ahead.

All the other dreams appeared to be connected. Ada's experiences in Merida provided a retrospective insight into the "badly shattered mirror" as pertaining to the image she once had of herself as "a good Christian girl," a former strict believer of certain church rules and practices which governed her life, as well as biases against other religions lacking knowledge of the" right truths" or "the only true church" which only her religion had. The many ripe, colored fruits reflected the teachings to which she would be exposed as well as her willingness to receive and be nourished by them. The fruits were ripe and ready to be eaten just as Ada was ripe and ready to learn the new teachings and to absorb and be nourished by them. At first the learning would be slow, as in her dream of walking, but the pace and volume of learning would develop, as in her "high speed running," into a wider exposure and deeper growth in spirituality through her avid reading pursuits. Her success in being granted a sabbatical leave as well as earning American citizenship could also have been among references to the ripe, colorful fruits.

After much thought, Ada realized that the "particular star" in the sky that was very bright was predictive of her meeting with her dear friend Sarah, who would initiate and generously introduce her into a new spiritual world. Of all the experiences Ada had in the city of Merida in the Yucatan, her encounter with Sarah to this day remains a shining, rare, beautiful, and incomparable gift. It was as if Sarah was specially prepared by the Universe for their encounter at the party where this tall, graceful Canadian lady, among all the other many unfamiliar guests gathered there, walked towards Ada, a stranger, and asked if she could share her table. How synchronous, beautiful, and incredible was that moment!

The dream where she entered an unusual house proved the most challenging to unravel, yet it became quite fascinating. It is possible that the house represented

Ada with her many aspects. But why Chinese tapestry, worn shoes, green walking shoes, oversized at first, then later too small? Again, the "star" Sarah, led Ada to the teachings of the Orient symbolized by Chinese tapestry, something beautifully woven as were the informative teachings. She not only read Indian mystic Yogananda's spiritually enriching book, *Autobiography of a Yogi,* but took his mind-expanding course on *Self-Realization,* which led her deeper into Buddhist teachings, the Tao, and other Eastern philosophies. But worn shoes? They seemed to suggest that she needed to let go of some old, time-worn beliefs she had journeyed with, practiced, used for protection, and felt religiously secure in for so long, and held to be beyond question. Beliefs of the only true church, rules about confession and sin, might have served their purpose for some time by restricting her thinking and capacity to question, but she must now be released from their choking grip to accommodate the light of new, liberating understanding, such as the concepts of Oneness, Unity, interconnectedness, and Laws of the Universe. The "oversized green leather walking shoes" dream signified the new lasting knowledge of rejuvenation (green), which she acquired from Sarah, although it did seem contrary and overwhelming at first (oversized). However, it led to further traveling and forays into other teachings from various other spiritual masters thus accelerating a change and growth in consciousness for Ada. The experience was green compared to the darkness, frustration, and desert period Ada had not so long ago experienced! For Ada, Cayce's analysis of dreams as being "a self-regulating, self-enhancing, self-training program" was being realized through a step by step process. She felt like an onion being stripped layer by layer and very slowly.

The dream which had the most striking effect on Ada in the above series, was the dream about two exotic birds. These dreams occurred early in the Spring of 1990 before the summer and her sabbatical year experiences in the Fall. Without recognizing any relationship with the dream, at an unexpected invitation in the summer, Ada abruptly decided, with the help of a loan, to join a group on a European tour of several countries, and visited many famous cities she had read about in history in elementary school, such as London, Brussels, Berne, and the rivers, the Rhine and Danube. In Rome, she pinched herself standing in St. Peter's Square and the famous Vatican Cathedral, center of Catholicism. Then her jaw dropped at the sight of the imposing structure of the Coliseum of gladiator fame; Venice and Florence she recalled were intimately connected with famous Shakespeare plays as well as renowned artists and sculptors; France, with religious architecture, such as the famous Notre Dame Cathedral and the gardens and palace of Napoleon Bonaparte. As if to embellish the gift she was given, a rich English lady with whom she became friendly on the tour, invited Ada to have tea with her on the sidewalk of the Champs de Elysses with full view of the Triumphal Arch and a parade in action with full colors, pomp and circumstance to boot! Ada wondered if she was dreaming in broad daylight with eyes wide open! She had to pinch herself again! Was it all a reality or illusion? These places certainly provided an out-of-this-world exotic experience that Ada could not have imagined!

That experience was followed by the journey to Merida in the Yucatan which is already described. Both adventures were aptly predicted and symbolized as "two exotic birds," indicating on one level the flying experiences involved, as well as the inner soaring of spirit Ada would feel.

This retrospective view brought to mind Ada's first recurring dream of climbing a rock, bruised, bleeding, and without progress. Her efforts to advance spiritually were then being retarded and increasingly led to inner stagnation and restlessness, a kind of bruising and bleeding. Change occurred, as she responded to a compulsion, a daring new climb, an upward progression, an inner drive to explore and resolve what Sarah Breathnach refers to as "the yearning for Something

More," to appease the stifling sensation from within despite Ada's former façade of "all is well."

Each person's life path is as "individual as a fingerprint", according to Cayce. Without awareness, influences by external events labeled as hallmarks of "success" in a mundane world, can steer us off the track that is ours to follow. The dreams had been signposts all along with messages Ada neglected because she was too blind to see, became too inept by disempowering beliefs, and too preoccupied to listen or to question. Perhaps she was too "involved with doing, having, and making, instead of being"[4] as Praagh so succinctly captures. Thanks to a merciful and generous universe which kept beckoning, reminding, and gently prodding her through her dreams!

Dreams, such as the one about the exotic birds occurring long before Ada thought of, or even planned two international trips, are referred to as predictive by many famous dream authors, such as Sylvia Browne, Dr. Judith Orloff, and Edgar Cayce. Similar to the dream of two spaceships described in Series A, this predictive quality seemed to characterize many of Ada's subsequent dreams and will later be given more focus.

Dreams in the Sabbatical Year Continued-
The Middle Phase – SERIES C

- *I give an impromptu speech and I am surprisingly told, "Congratulations!"*
- *I am looking at a flower and it expands its bloom immediately right before my eyes!*
- *A huge rat tries to run in the opposite direction from me. I chase and kill it.*
- *I am driving with two others and pass over some huge rocks rather smoothly. Then I take a perpendicular path as though it were a vertical*

> *wall. I feel a great deal of support from the right – unbelievable, all the way up until I reach the top where the view is a beautiful plain. What a relief when I get there!*
> - *I am standing in a huge laundry room. All the fixtures are in white; the people working there are all white and dressed in white clothing.*
> - *My maternal grandmother, Ada appears; she looks young, beautiful, and dressed in white.*

Ada believed that this series gave further assurance by reflecting some repeated symbols and themes, such as being congratulated, a flower opening, and going over a rock. Perhaps Ada's avid interests were being given approval, and a flower, again expanding its bloom, represented her receptivity and growth into new truths which she found inspiring. Why a rat, a threatening symbol, which she chased and killed? Did she have an enemy which she overcame? Perhaps the enemy was her own fears, doubts, procrastination, or guilt from "leaving the Church" at least temporarily to explore new knowledge.

Contrary to bruising and bleeding she endured in her previous rock dream, "passing over huge rocks smoothly" and getting firm support along a direct, upward path to a beautiful place, should have erased any doubts Ada might have had about being on the right track in her explorations. Yet, the question remained: what would this path be like, and when would it appear? Apparently, there was a need for more patience while uncertainty flourished! It was a sabbatical year when Ada was intensely engaged in reading works of spiritual masters and taking time out for recreational activities.

Then, as if to give further assistance, one helper on her support staff was her favorite, strong Grandma! But why was the dreamer in a laundry room? Could it be that Ada was being cleansed, purified, rebirthed, prepared for something which necessitated purity of spirit? The meaning of these dreams, in addition to those listed below in Series D would remain subtle, baffling, and would not be thoroughly revealed for a long time.

Dreams in the Sabbatical Year: The Final Phase – SERIES D

- *I am ascending some steps. Figures dressed in white are passing me up and down and I am being helped to the top. On one side there is a mountain and a beautiful valley with a breathtaking scene dominated by a church.*

- *I feel a sharp, long needle thrust into my left breast. The middle of my two palms are gouged and bleeding. I wake up with my heart racing.*

- *I am standing in a pastureland. A beautiful, pure white horse with a gorgeous, fluffy mane gallops towards me and places its two front hoofs in my upturned palms. The touch is so gentle, I barely feel it. There is a moment of silent communication as our eyes meet. I awake in awe and with a feeling of deep peace.*

- *I enter a house and there is a strong smell of ripe bananas. Someone leads me to the cellar where I meet my friend Agatha, who with a smile, places six ripe, speckled, sweet smelling ripe bananas in my hand. I wake up smelling a strong scent of ripe bananas around me.*

- *I hold a little girl of two years in my arms, introduce her to some friends, then we climb up the side stair of a house to the top. I say to her, "This is better," referring to the space at the top of the house. The view is beautiful.*

- *I am riding a bike up a steep hill. Two tall men from behind put me with my bike in a truck as if I am as light as feather and take me to the top of the hill.*

The dreams in this series appeared to echo more support and love expressed by "figures dressed in white," "a pure white horse," with silent communication of peace, being lifted out of difficulty while "biking up a steep hill," or the gift of "speckled ripe bananas" from a dear friend. Ada initially assigned the support and love to the influence of the wonderful spiritual authors whose works she had been reading, but later realized that she needed to dig deeper. Perhaps that is why she went lower to the "cellar," her subconscious, to receive answers. In what way were the sweet-smelling, luscious bananas significant? They symbolized reward or more fruits of the spirit to be realized!

Her analysis of the second dream was also another example of her short-sighted understanding of clues on her journey. Being jabbed with a needle in her breast and having bleeding palms immediately conveyed imminent harm from an external source, and she should be on the alert. But this was only an awareness which veiled the layers of meaning which would be revealed according to contexts which would later evolve and be explained.

Although limited, the interpretive insights into all the above dreams served to strengthen the foundation for Ada to begin to understand the impact of subsequent dreams. The themes of support in difficult circumstances, suffering, growth, encouragement, and beauty in many forms were recurring patterns in the lists of dreams before and during Ada's sabbatical year. It seemed that these themes became the vehicles through which Ada would experience the change which would eventually steer her along the archaeological pathways of her being, providing clues towards her real "blooming" foreshadowed years earlier by the begonia blossoms!

The interpretive insights also provided the encouragement Ada needed to begin to understand more fully, the dreams which she continued to have during her career. She realized that one dominant repetitive clue in her digging which required greater scrutiny was "upward movement" expressed as climbing stairs, biking up a steep hill, moving along a perpendicular path. For more clarity regarding the clues and themes of the dreams in Series C and D, Ada decided to examine more carefully, two pathways that were intertwining on a new level: her professional career and her spiritual life. Since Ada had learned new truths, had undergone some measure of inner change, how did she function as she continued her career?

CHAPTER NINE

A dream is the mirror of the soul bringing us a clear view of ourselves and the learning situations in which we are involved. Those dreams are quite revealing in content showing us aspects of ourselves we hadn't noticed...revealing how we think we appear opposed to how we really are. Tanner[1]

By understanding themselves and putting that understanding into action, they live more authentic, productive, and rewarding lives. When their behavior reflects who they really are, they feel a sense of integrity, a greater oneness with their soul and spirit. Barrick.[2]

DREAMS ALONG INTERTWINING PATHWAYS

A s previously mentioned, after Ada returned from a year's sabbatical, she emotionally re-entered the world of work as if alighting from another planet. The next five years, September 1991 to Fall 1996 would be a period best described as filled with challenges and changes.

In one way, her dream experiences and new found knowledge had been catalysts for unforeseen inner changes, a shift which initially gave her a feeling of being there, yet somehow feeling apart from her surroundings; in another way, work was a relief as she thought that delving back into academic activities would provide a new focus and mental distractions which would at least ground her into reality and lessen the frequency of her dreams. Her thoughts couldn't have been more far removed from the reality to follow. She didn't have the slightest inkling of the manner in which she would be driven by people and circumstances, within, yet outside her control, and what she would accomplish as a result of them, always against the backdrop of dreams.

Despite the challenges, the next five years after returning to work would also be analogous to a process of being carried along the tide of a river with smooth as well as turbulent rapids.

In their predictive wisdom, her dreams continued to give her messages expressing the imminent physical, mental, and emotional challenges, solace, and triumphs to which, at the time, she had given only scant attention. It was as though they were a separate domain of her life to be attended to later. There were more pressing issues commanding her focus. However, she continued to faithfully record her dreams.

Quite revealing was a retrospective look at some of the various professional activities and contexts during the period, 1991-1996..

CHAPTER TEN

Don't try and play someone else's role; play your own...Knowing yourself is the source of change for your life. We change our reality by changing what is within us. This is our place of wholeness. Praagh[1]

...So in the mistakes as well as in the victories we forge our Christhood. That's why it takes time to become Christlike because you become that by free will or by experience. Barrick[2]

TEACHING AND OTHER
EXTRA-CURRICULAR ACTIVITIES

I n addition to her teaching load, Ada worked with several wonderful colleagues to foster sharing of expertise and scholarship through academic conferences under the banner of two organizations which she chaired at different periods. Needless to say, this required time-consuming meetings and planning, most of which had rewarding outcomes.

A common expression in the university environment is "publish or perish," but that was a minor motivating factor for Ada. As she continued to inspire her students on many levels, their responses in turn challenged her to reinforce or modify her strategies. She found some of those experiences valuable enough to be expressed in publications and shared with colleagues at local and international conferences.

As a result of her work, she found out by coincidence that she may be eligible for a promotion that would require decision making and evaluation processes spanning at least two years at various levels of college governance.

During these years of demanding educational activity, Ada's fervor for new spiritual teachings continued and seemed to have supplied a strange energy for her work in an uncanny way. It seemed for the most part, she was unaware of the extent to which this was occurring while caught in the web of responsibilities. In the meantime, the predictive dreams continued to send their messages; Ada again faithfully recorded them then put her journal to rest until the next dream event.

It has been said that it is not the destination that matters, it is the journey. So it was with Ada, who now in her senior years, tried to visit and place her recordings in categories, with two major intentions: first, to emphasize that it was not so much the goal of an uncertain promotion that was so significant; rather, it was the impact of subtle, unknown forces that were at work in her on the dream journey towards achieving that goal; this was not then at a conscious level of Ada's awareness. Second, to show the relationship between her professional and spiritual life as they progressively intertwined on her incredible, transformative journey. The dreams and their themes seemed to reflect the overlap directing her activities and the related circumstances.

Dreams and Themes

Edgar Cayce contends that each person's way of dreaming is as individual as his fingerprint, or as the markings of his soul in its long journey through many lives, and comments further that interpretations ought to be done "in the light of his whole body of recorded dreams, rather than shooting at one dream at a time... seeing how a given theme repeats itself in a series of dreams."[3].

Some of the symbols in the previous series of dreams continued to recur in addition to new ones, as shown in the following Series arranged according to themes.

Challenges and Encouragement- SERIES E

- *I am climbing a steep hill pulling one large, and one small load*
- *I am climbing a steep hill pulling two loads*
- *Two children appear and are joined at the thighs*
- *A ball is thrown to me from a distance and I catch it*

- *A ball is thrown in a lake; I swim to reach it; it eludes me then I finally grab it*
- *I am climbing a steep hill and I meet beautiful colored birds on the way up*
- *I look across on a window ledge where there are beautiful colored birds. One comes into my room, lands in my arms and allows me to pat it.*
- *I am climbing a straight fragile, perpendicular tree. As it sways back and forth I feel fear but I keep on climbing until I reach a point far beyond a landing. Then someone calls my name.*
- *Some Asian and dark-skinned people are working in an orange grove. A man guides me over a hill pointing to where I want to go. Is it East Scotland? From the roof of a house, he jumps down and I follow. The owner comes, greets us, and says, "Just tell me where you want to go and I'll take you."*
- *Women bring me gifts of fruit; among them are huge, juicy oranges.*

Ada recognized that she no more encountered the rock symbol in her dreams. What was being repeated was "climbing a steep hill" or climbing a tree, being guided over a hill or "pulling two loads." At this point in her career, she was writing two peer-reviewed journal articles. Again, as in the previous series of dreams, Ada was climbing and reaching for something else, not yet clearly discernible, but she continued to respond to an inner drive and direction. Her mind was being occupied in a productive way, creatively exploring, daring, and expressing. The significance of "two" referred not only to "loads" of writing, but to workshops in which she was involved. She was making progress despite the difficulty represented by the steepness of the hill. A ball, an object thrown to her was caught. Another ball, even though it eluded her at first, as she swam across the lake, she retrieved it, which pointed to a "successful" achievement of those goals. The theme of reaching for something higher seemed to be repeated in the climb of the tree, that is, the movement from one set of activities to another, caught in the tide of professional demands and spiritual experiences, urging her to a landing in a high area.

Did Ada have messengers of good news? Her continuous bird symbol answered positively. She must have been nourished and guided spiritually by the symbols of fruits and a house owner who lived "over a hill" and who expressed eagerness to help –"just tell me where you want to go and I will take you." The hill, climb, and roof appeared to be symbols of elevation. However, Ada was then uncertain of where "I will take you" meant, but was revealed later as being beyond anything she could have imagined.

The dig continued, but to where was it leading? Where will it end? The *what* and *when* of her dreams were being excavated, but clues to the *why*? Could that be the meaning of "tell me where you want to go and I will take you?" Was this on a professional or a spiritual level? Ada had no inkling of the perfect answer, but during the dig, she kept in mind Cayce's idea of several levels of meaning in some dreams, and that they are a "self-regulating, self-enhancing, self-training program over which the dreamer's own soul presides" and that "the dreamer is central to the process. " It is not the dream that must be interpreted, it is the dreamer, Cayce also advised. If that is so, the dream and the dreamer are inextricably linked, which meant Ada had much to learn about herself as reflected in her dreams.

In the next category of dreams, Ada seemed to be receiving inspiration, joy, peace, and beauty from other agents of support as the juxtaposition of academic and spiritual experiences continued to unfold and became more demanding for scrutiny.

Again according to Cayce, a new experience dream "adds to the permanent repertoire of the dreamer...once the psyche opened the door to a particular type of dreaming, it seems to program a series of such dreams to train the dreamer."[4]. Whereas in previous dreams, climbing was dominant, this category of dreams seemed to emphasize the theme of music which has been the foremost medium among Ada's most appealing forms of entertainment. She still climbed "a flight of stairs" or "a hill covered with flowers", but when she was not hearing instrumental or vocal harmonious music from others, she also played professionally, at times "far beyond my abilities," and encountered children, water, and animals. But what was the real significance of music for Ada? Why were new symbols now being expressed in her dreams?

Inspiration, Joy, Peace, and Beauty – SERIES F:

- *Several voices are singing rich music in parts; someone is playing the guitar and children are singing.*
- *I run up a tall flight of stairs to a room where I listen to beautiful organ music played by a woman.*
- *I climb a hill covered with flowers.*
- *I am looking at a place constructed with two circular levels, each trimmed with white lacy frills. Music is being played on both levels.*
- *I play the piano with a professional style far beyond my abilities.*
- *I am given a beautiful pink dress, pink shoes and handbag; I am in a living room with pink couches.*
- *A woman plays skillfully on the piano but she seems shy.*
- *Two groups of children and adults are singing in rich harmonies while I am caressing a cow behaving erratically while it is giving birth.*
- *I am swimming in deep water.*

- ***There is a lake and the water is clear; there is a stream with mineral qualities running into it.***
- ***A large white swan gracefully walks on a lawn in front of me.***
- ***I am cuddling a puppy; I give it a bath and it starts speaking to me.***
- ***There is a celebration in a building and the decorations are all white. There is beautiful music upstairs and downstairs.***

Beyond sensations of inspiration, joy, and beauty, Connie Kaplan provides an interesting insight by stating, "when you hear music in your dream, you experience a profound healing" and at the level of healing, "we become attuned to the level of soul and we become the instrument of the Divine...allowing ourselves to be played and thus healed."[5] This is indeed profound, and Ada yearned to understand the role of her dreams in her capacity to be played and healed!

About the time of these dreams, Ada recalled and recorded a strange experience which occurred on her way to work one morning. She had just turned the corner of a huge church less than a block from the main entrance of her workplace. Ada somehow felt as though she was lifted off the ground and carried to the main entrance of the building. It was as though she was walking as usual yet not walking! "Dear God, am I losing my mind?" she privately wondered. She thought of it as a weird, uncanny, yet possibly real experience. After arriving in her office, as she closed the door, she felt strangely peaceful, but she sat for a while in silence, her head on her desk, trying to assess and convince herself that she was sober and normal, and was her usual self. She had to be, as she was sure she had not taken any mind altering drug or medication, did not hit the liquor bottle, and no alien herb had been absorbed in her body. She finally summoned her courage, adopted a camouflage, stepped out the door wearing a normal face and the even steps of a very normal person hoping that anyone she met would register just that.

Ada often wondered whether that incident was illustrative of being "attuned to the level of soul," and "allowing ourselves to be played and thus healed." Other symbols of healing, joy, and inspiration during Ada's professional struggles included the healing water she swam in, the "stream with mineral qualities," as well as the elegant, white swan which passed by her on the lawn. The majestic swan, seemed so different from the birds in her previous dreams, but nevertheless, one which she regarded as a special gift, a spiritually uplifting symbol. Flowers, matching accessories of pink, white, lacy frills were other symbols which she concluded to refer to the dedication of her service in the projects she had undertaken. The help she gave to a "cow behaving erratically while giving birth" or nurturing to a speaking puppy which she lovingly cuddled also seemed to refer to the struggle and careful attention to details necessary for the tedious requirements and goals for promotion to be fulfilled.

Elation and Upward Movement – SERIES G

- *I am being pulled up, up, up through clouds; I look at the scene below and I think, "How beautiful!" I feel suspended and others are floating with me.*

- *Elegant horses are riding the clouds! I run up some steep steps to a recreation area to get a good view of them.*

- *A brick tower stretches toward the sky; I am inside and I am pointing to the sky.*

- *I am in the company of young Chinese girls.*

- *Two figures dressed in white are conversing; they call me, and as I approach them I have the feeling that I am being given an opportunity for something.*

- ***I am dancing to a waltz in circular fashion at a party.***
- ***Young Asian children surround me.***

For quite a while, intermittently, Ada was unsure whether her experience of "being carried along" in her work circumstances was real or she had temporarily taken leave of her senses. She realized that sometimes when one is alone in a certain set of personal circumstances, it is best and safer to continue to embrace them in silence and private wonder, playing with, pondering, and savoring the mystery or the madness of it all. In that space and time, she felt as though there was no one she could confide in without fear of being ridiculed, viewed as abnormal or a misfit, (as she was once labeled); it didn't seem possible to approach anyone one who could fully grasp her often inexplicable inner world of events. Sylvia Browne did wisely warn that spiritual development is a "very isolated period," a "crisis of faith" and different from anything experienced before, "but you certainly know when you are in it. It's like birth pains." Ada wasn't sure what was really being born in her. Her only choice was to allow herself to quietly go with the flow of whatever was occurring. She had no choice but to continue to experience it alone.

In the meantime, there were colleagues who analyzed her as "difficult to know, or different," and they were probably right. At that stage, even in her adult years, Ada's knowledge of herself was still in its infancy, swerving from normal to questionable or out of balance.

The above dreams representing elation and upward movement were no less mind-boggling. She often woke up wondering if during sleep she had unknowingly at any time taken physical leave of her bed, yet sometimes feeling strangely happy. Why can't the language of dreams be more direct, especially those like Ada's? Dreams are a" self-regulating program," Cayce stated. In this heroic dig, who was Ada becoming? She was being changed but into what? But *Why*! "Be patient, Ada, remember you are undergoing "self-training;" you are in a "self-regulating program," stated an inner voice. Ada hardly knew what she was training herself in, to become what, or which program she was then regulating. But the dig had to continue. There was no turning back!

The upward movement motif was repeated in two of the above dreams: "pulled up, up, up" and "run up some steep steps." A third found Ada pointing skyward; yet another, waltz dancing at a party. Was that indicating a view of something higher and a state of joy which she should always cultivate? Although Cayce pointed out that dreams carry significant meanings on several levels at once and should be interpreted accordingly, Ada at this time, believes that all these dreams had an elusive spiritual link which was reinforced by the two figures in white who conversed and called her.

But where exactly does growth in spirituality take an individual so unsure of herself? No two individuals' experiences along the journey are identical. Experiences shape who we become, but to what extent do experiences direct us to our best selves? On the importance of self-evaluation, Breathnach refers to Emily Hancock's view that"...we sense that something is missing in our lives and fruitlessly search 'out there' for the answers. What's often wrong is that we are disconnected from an authentic sense of self"[6] . If going "inside" is the right direction, how long is it before anyone comes to a resting place of deep confident knowing of having arrived at the level of "the authentic sense of self?" And what is this authentic sense of self anyway? Ada queried as her inner world of dreams was forcing her to explore unfamiliar, neglected regions within herself, sensing that clues to the answer lay ahead somewhere in the exploration. Zukav explains that authenticity occurs when the personality and soul are in alignment. On the dream journey, Ada searched to find clues related to her degree of alignment. How would she know when her personality and soul are aligned, and authentically? The digging must continue.

It was after the predictive dream about the two figures in white that Ada had the privilege of meeting two courageous spiritual teachers. Norma Milanovich, a former educator, became a vessel for channeling by the Ascended Master Kuthumi, whose service to the planet entailed using specially dictated rites to open various closed portals on planet earth to accommodate new universal energies for positive change. Ada was fortunate to have traveled with her to some of the world locations and participated in the spiritual ceremonies.

Learning that individuals can use energy to heal rather than hurt others, was another special gift Ada received from Del Pe`, a highly trained spiritual teacher from the Orient, indicated by Asian children in her dreams. His oriental healing teachings appealed to many in New York City where Ada attended and benefited from many of his sessions. Ada was convinced that being dressed in white denoted the high level and qualities of spiritual devotion and service offered by the two messengers. In their presence, Ada was always conscious of a feeling of elation, and she was convinced that she was being transformed somehow by their presence and teaching. Perhaps she was being "pulled up, up, up" after all.

Another unforgettable encounter was with Scotch teacher Benjamin Crème, who visited the United States bringing spiritual truths beyond religion. One night, previous to meeting him the next day, Ada had this dream:

> *I am standing at the corner of an intersection, then I leap into the air and land far into the next block. My heart feels as though it has swollen much larger than its normal size.*

In a meditation circle the following day, Ada had the privilege of sitting next to Benjamin while all in the group faced his special instrument, the tetrahedron. Arranged in a circle, the group joined hands during the meditation. From Mr. Creme's hand, Ada felt a surge of hot energy moving from his hand to hers, then a current to her body. Ada later realized that the experience was a gift related to her dream the night before. As a result of the gift, her spirit was uplifted, ("leap into the air"), and her heart became swollen ("larger than its normal size").

Again, without totally realizing the really true meaning and impact of her dreams of *Elation and Upward Movement*, she was in some uncanny way being "pulled up, up, up through the clouds," to other unknown levels of herself yet to be discovered and understood.

Adding to her spiritual adventures was her attendance at the 40th anniversary of Universal Articulate Interdimensional Understanding of Science (UNARIUS), a center for the study of Reincarnation in San Diego, Mexico. The seeds for this new experience on reincarnation were already sown years earlier when Ada met Sarah during her visit to Merida in the Yucatan. There in San Diego, she had encounters with some extraordinary people who expanded her knowledge of the multidimensional structure of the cosmos, its myriad and varied dwellers, the influence of Space Brothers and the interplay of science and spirituality. This missing link is only now igniting new curiosity among scholars in current explorations for further understanding of man and the universe. Without realizing it, the above experiences seemed to indicate that Ada was really undergoing "self-regulating" and "self-training" through further exposure to new spiritual knowledge.

Despite her many dreams of elation, elevation, joy, and beauty, there were those that were frightening, wounding, and disheartening.

Limitation, Lack, Adversity – SERIES H

- *I am daubed with dirt.*
- *I kill some small rats and wound a large one which is joined by another. I run from them.*
- *I wet my bed. A male comes to lie beside me and I am embarrassed but he pays no attention to that. He brings antiques to furnish my room.*
- *I am supposed to play the organ for a church service but I cannot find the music for "Holy, Holy, Holy."*
- *A black snake attacks a woman, bites her and she is bleeding. A larger, longer one comes towards me and I feel its powerful fangs in my flesh; I pray to the Buddha and I escape.*
- *My lost pocketbook is returned to me by a stranger.*
- *I have just put gas in the old car but it won't start.*
- *I enter a building covered with cobwebs; I call someone ahead of me about them; I sweep one set away and I am getting others to do the same.*

During the years 1991 to late 1994, Ada's dreams were interspersed with dreams of limitation, lack, and adversity. Two repeated symbols which Ada became convinced to be representing negativity, animosity, or emotional harm were rats and snakes. In a previously described dream, a rat showed itself, then ran in the opposite direction from Ada. She interpreted that to be her fears and guilt which resulted after changing her religious beliefs. Also, in other previous dreams, she had killed and wounded rats. However, in Series H above, she had to escape from their overpowering and threatening approach. Her dream of the black snake was even more ominous when an unrecognized woman near her was bitten and bleeding, while Ada herself felt the "powerful fangs" of another snake in her flesh. Ada now believes that the woman, as well as the male who overlooked her embarrassment and furnished her room, were ones who supported her in her professional endeavors. The dream of being "daubed with dirt" connected with the threat of rats and snake with "powerful fangs in her flesh," and connoted the negative emotions around her of insults, criticisms, and put downs, some of which occurred during and after the process of aspiring for a promotion.

More Reflections on Dreams in Series H!

Ada grew up in a peaceful, humble home where respect for everyone, young, old, poor and rich was fostered. It was a way of life for her parents who expected the same from their children. She believed she would bring dishonor to them and guilt to herself, if she had insulted anyone in ways she had experienced especially from those whom she was fond of. Since her strategy of non-retaliation or respectful communication did not improve the situation with some of her attackers, emotional distancing became her means of protection. Frequently ringing in her ears were her mother's reminders in her childhood from the book of Proverbs 16:32, "He that is slow to anger is better than the mighty; and he that ruleth his spirit better than he that taketh a city. " From Proverbs 15:1 she would quote, "The Lord is close to the broken hearted and saves those who are crushed in spirit;" a third on her list of sayings was, "A soft answer turneth away wrath, but grievous words stir up anger." Isaiah 65:5. Dad's favorite admonition which he often sternly repeated to his children was, "If you know better, do better." Ada was not inclined to compromise those as among her cherished her values.

She "could not find the music;" "the car would not start" although it had enough gas, seemed to represent her insecurity and lack of safety. But more than that, those dreams revealed her stifled abilities at times to joyfully and effectively execute some of her professional duties in that environment. Thanks to her students who kept her engaged and sane during class sessions.

In the above dreams, it is interesting that Ada was able to escape after praying to the Buddha; then, something she valued, perhaps recognition of her dedication, represented by her "lost pocketbook was returned by a stranger" was expressed again by the help of others whom she called on to sweep away cobwebs of confusion and resentment.

In her exploration, Ada became convinced that the woman bitten, and the generous, compassionate male were supporters working behind the scenes as benefactors in her endeavors. An even more intriguing aspect of the male who entered her room was that he disregarded her wet bed, a symbol of embarrassment and vulnerability, and instead, furnished her room with antiques, that is, giving her valuable assistance and intervention, perhaps working as an instrument of the Buddha to whom she had prayed. In other words, the male responded to her call to help "sweep away the cobwebs," of obstruction to make the way clear.

Some Paradoxes

What seemed so striking to Ada, was that despite the various degrees of adversity, she continued to have dreams of inspiration, upward movement, and healing music. It seemed unseen forces were around her as if acting as buffers helping her to heal and endure emotional pain. She was still being "carried along" some turbulent torrents in her life journey. Those dream patterns did not occur just once, leave their message for Ada to resolve, and then leave. No, the adventures on the journey to the wherever of the *why* of her dreams were significant despite the feeling of being in a foreign zone of herself. The dreams of upward movement continued, so did repetitions of music, flowers and fruits.

As recorded by Sechrist, Cayce stated that "love not only helps bear part of another's burden, but it also spans the dimensions of time and space."[7]. This idea seemed to be clearly verified in the following dreams in Series I.

Themes of Love, Protection, and Visits from the Other Side – SERIES I

- *Mom is standing by an open door, and she smilingly invites me to go in. The place is filled with light. We walk briefly together, but I see nothing, then I am alone.*

- *Mom and Gran are conversing and laughing while seated on a bench in a garden with hanging flowers all around.*

- *I visit Master who lies sick in a decorated room. He hugs, kisses me, and whispers in my ear that he has something for me. "I found a mate for you," he says. (In Canada, I once attended a lecture given by Indian Master Gurinder Singh).*

- *Mom hugs and kisses me on the lips. (Repeated in many other dreams.)*

- *Dad walks with a smile toward me. He looks healthy, and young. We hug.*

- *A choir is singing beautiful harmonies being conducted by Dad. I wait until he is finished, then I hold his hand and together we walk to an elevated platform, where I ask, "Shall we dance?" Dad, smiling, moves gracefully.*

- *I am sitting with guests at a dining table. Mom comes, stretches over, and kisses me on the lips! She is gorgeous, dressed beautifully with keeled hat, lipstick and angelic smile. She sits in a chair set for her.*
- *Two dear friends, Philomena and Hilda visit, and they are laughing merrily.*

Love spanning time and space is truly a beautiful way to view the above dreams, but at the time they occurred, Ada always gave thanks for the visits and felt delighted that her parents and friends were happy occupying their room in "the many mansions."

What she found astounding was that in her growing up years, she was never kissed or hugged by Mom or Dad although there was never any doubt that she felt their love! But in the years 1994 to 1996 during this time of stress, challenge, and uncertainty, Ada received repeated dream experiences of being visited, hugged, even kissed on the lips by her Mom as if to give healing, comfort, and confidence. Dad, who also while alive was never physically expressive of his love, joined in giving healing visits! He was definitely part of the love squad, as were two other dear laughing friends.

One of the dreams that Ada found very puzzling was when Mom smilingly invited Ada to enter an open door where there was light and walked with her as if introducing her to something. Was this supposed to be a space without worry, with accessibility to happiness indicated by the light? In another dream, even a Buddhist Master whom Ada once met in Canada, showered his affection and had something to tell her – he found a mate for her! Who could that mate be? A soul mate? The answer was left "blowing in the wind" as Ada continued her dig through *What* and *When* aiming to reach the *Why*.

Edgar Cayce emphasized that the power of love could break through the veil of separation....love uniting with love, making connections, bridging the divide. It seems that the intention of such expressions of love in her dreams was to provide comfort, hope, healing, and give assistance while jumping the hurdles. Mom's kiss on Ada's lips and invitation through a door, Gran's smiling visit among flowers, a Master's promise of a gift, were all expressions of love which should have given Ada cause for outer expression of joy. They probably did, but as passing moments.

Instead, the rigorous requirements and uncertain process of obtaining the status of full professor in her Division occupied her mind to the extent that the meaning and impact of the above uplifting dreams were for the most part, at the time, again, lost to her awareness. Despite the questionable existence of another world within herself, the urge to record them never waned.

In his book, Harmon Bro comments on the importance Cayce placed on knowing the purpose of a dream in order to interpret it, and states that the psyche tries to supply what is most needed by the dreamer. Ada had been given dreams of inspiration, joy, healing, love, and warnings of lack and limitation. One way then to understand the *Why* was to recognize that love from many sources had been operating in her favor, sometimes in unusual ways, behind the scenes, yet undoubtedly present and guiding her along the rough tracks on her journey. With that solution, couldn't the dig end right there? Not quite! With such premature action there would have been a loss of the most exciting part leading to the WHY which still lay in the dig far ahead!

CHAPTER ELEVEN

Take the time to discover your real intentions...if your real situation is to create harmony instead of discord, cooperation instead of competition, sharing instead of hoarding, reverence for life instead of exploitation, act on it, because it is an intention of love and can create only healthy and wholesome consequences. Zukav [1]

SELECTED CULMINATING
DREAMS AND SYMBOLS

The period preceding final decisions regarding Ada's aspirations for promotion were crucial. There were rigorous criteria to be fulfilled, as magnified scrutiny at the final level of governance in the matter was inevitable. During this period, the years 1995 and 1996, Ada recorded the following profusion of dreams, each of which she believed was only meant to reinforce the other in significance.

The Repetition of Two – Series I

Frequently, Ada dreamed of two in several ways. Below are a few expressions.

- *Two bright orange goldfish are swimming in a bowl*
- *Two young children are engaged in a musical performance: a girl is playing the piano and a boy sings like a professional;*
- *I am given two keys and I use one to open one side of a two-door cabinet*
- *I am lying on my back, and two large golden ducklings are playing with each other on my chest!*
- *I am speeding along a smooth, wet road. I make a U-turn and drive in the opposite direction.*
- *I am in the company of two light-skinned, blonde haired women*

In terms of positive messages regarding the activities, two of the dreams should receive special mention. While Ada was actively organizing a conference, she wrote two journal articles which were accepted and were soon to be published, and her second academic book was near completion. The dream of the two keys referred to two aspects of a conference being planned. Funding which Ada applied for to offset the cost of the conference was provided through a granting institution, so that one door to the cabinet was opened by one key. Why was the second key not used to open the second door? This was explained in a later dream where she was "speeding along a smooth, wet road" then made a hairpin turn in the opposite direction from which she came. The speaker Ada selected was voted down as inappropriate for that conference. Like the turn of a hairpin, the process returned to where it began, finding a new speaker. These dreams occurred long before the related events.

One morning Ada received in the mail, copies of two glowing letters of recommendation which were sent to administrative personnel involved in the promotion process. Ada received copies of the letters the day after dreaming about "two light-skinned women," two women with whom Ada had worked closely on some projects, thus confirming the last dream in Series I.

The Significance of Music – Series J

As mentione before, Connie Kaplan reminds us that "when you hear music in your dream you experience a profound healing."[2]. This is so true. It can be noted in the previous dream series, one of the recurring symbols in Ada's dreams was music.

Again, during this period, the prominence of music became even more evident. Ada recorded 'a body' of music dreams such as:

- *I hear beautiful music upstairs and downstairs in a house*
- *Strong, reverberating sounds are coming from an unusual instrument played by a little girl;*

- *I am playing the guitar with two others. I join them, first by guessing, then I strum solo the hymn, "Leaning on the Everlasting Arms" without knowing I could do it.!*
- *In a palatial home, richly adorned, I peer through a window and see an elderly man giving an exquisite piano performance.*
- *In a park, someone plays with both hands on an instrument with several keys. At different times, I am either player or listener-an elderly man sits nearby and is satisfied.*
- *In an English cathedral, with some friends, I join in a rich chorus of voices singing hymns in captivating tones.*
- *I hear the most beautiful harmony of voices from the upstairs of a house- I wish to join them. A tall, buxom woman comes down the stairs in my direction and says, "You've just begun to live your life!"*

After a dream with music, Ada often woke up feeling reinvigorated and soothed. She would often hear sounds still ringing in her ears without comprehending with certainty, the current or immediate application of each specific dream with its predictive implications. Music, whether instrumental or vocal, denotes harmony and peace, an elevation of spirit similar to the expression of the birds. The last dream provided a clue for Ada regarding future revelations, "You've just begun to live your life!" suggesting events to be anticipated. At the time they were recorded, Ada was oblivious of their messages, just as she was with other dreams of babies and children which brought brief interludes of personal joy and curiosity:

Babies and Children – SERIES K

- *A baby boy is smiling at me from the end of my bed; a doctor is taking tissues from the foreheads of two babies.*

- *I seem to have a baby but others are caring for it.*
- *A healthy, smiling baby boy is sitting on my left leg.*
- *A young boy approaches me with a basket of ripe bananas; I hold a Chinese or Japanese child in my arms. It smiles then speaks to me while its mother stands close by. Then another child comes close to me. I give a hug.*
- *A young male child about ten years, is looking at me through a glass partition in a building. He runs out and we embrace.*

Among all the dreams in this series, the second held the clearest meaning to Ada. She believed that the baby referred to the deliberations which were then in the hands of assigned groups involved in the promotion process, which in other words, was a delicate baby and "others are caring for it." However, in three of the dreams a baby boy smiling or giving Ada a hug seemed to reinforce a pleasant outcome of a current or imminent endeavor.

Birds – SERIES L

Consistent with the first dream which she had at age fifteen, and even years later, Ada continued to dream of birds, and she continues to enjoy them as her special friends and bringers of good news. However, in this later series, more pronounced are radiant colors and softness. The emphasis of two were predictive of two projects which Ada would later undertake.

- *I visit a school where* **small children give me cards designed with birds**
- *Two beautiful birds with high pointed orange crowns are perched on a branch*

- *In a garden, a small bird is hopping, and I am told it is a nightingale. I am holding another bird and loving its softness.*
- *Two beautiful, bright colored birds are joined by two others on a branch so close, they appear as two although there are four.*
- *Two white doves perch on a branch, and a third flies in and spreads it wings.*

In the last dream, the doves, symbols of peace, as with music, would be reflective of the change in her emotional state from frustration to a more tranquil, placid emerging stage of self-understanding.

Caring Women- SERIES M

Loving female friends became another theme suggesting to Ada that she was being protected and guided by them.

- *Some women in long white garments bring me gifts of huge juicy oranges. They are ascending steps with music and singing. I hear the hymn "Abide with me" but the last stanza is irregular.*
- *Bonnie, my dear friend, appears elegantly dressed in white with a golden cord around her waist.*
- *Many women are in white dresses, ankle length, and decorated with gold sequins.*
- *Margaret, Hilda, and Alicia, friends from the Other Side, are in a laughing party.*

Less Frequent Significant Symbols: Series N

Light

- *There is a light in my head and someone says, "This is your higher self." The light becomes a round object like a pearl and settles in the center of my left eye.*

Fire

- *I am in a burning building but I am not in danger. I am trying to put the fire out.*
- *Towering red flames are around me but I don't think I am in danger.*

These two categories of dreams seem to carry messages of transformation for Ada. A light, a symbol of wisdom changes to a pearl, a precious jewel of beauty which settles in her eye as if to direct her vision or way of looking at her life circumstances as being directed towards positive ends. The "burning building" and "towering red flames" indicated the negative emotions which Ada was gradually beginning to own within herself, emotions that needed cleansing and purifying through burning as also a form of release. What role do snow and flowers play in Ada's dreams at this time?

Snow

- *I am walking on a snow-clad sidewalk. I look through a house window and see tables with white decorations for a feast. A green bird rests quite a while on my shoulder.*

- *I look through a window and everywhere is high in snow. A little bird pops through an opening and several others scramble outside. I call someone to witness it. Then the snow melts.*
- *It is snowing outside and I sit and enjoy watching it as it falls.*

Flowers

- *I am in a long, winding procession holding flowers with tiny blossoms which look like heather.*
- *A woman in white, places branches with clusters of white bougainvillea in different areas. I have one cluster on a plate with water and marvel at how fresh it stays.*
- *I am standing on a large porch decorated with Easter lilies*

While snow represents something frozen, in this context, there are themes of peace, celebration, and enjoyment reinforced by the presence of birds. There is the dominance of white color, also repeated in the flowers. Again, Ada recorded these dreams, but only now recognizing their messages of peace that should have dominated her inner life.

Among the dreams in Series N, one of the most memorable is the first in the group below.

Driving, Flying, Climbing

- *After walking some distance, I lay under some trees where I am disturbed by some men. I continue uphill and arrive at a spot with poorly made buildings. They stand in my way for a higher climb. After hearing my predicament, a woman points to a steep wall and says, "Use your fifty senses. Knock and you will hear the sound." I begin to knock and a man appears at another spot. In the tall steepness of the hill he opens a section revealing a stairway. I follow as he runs up the steps. At the top is a beautiful scenery of wide open spaces, distant hills, mountains, roads, and people working.*

- *I am driving but I am uncertain about the car's safety. A young man, about 18, gives me tips. I wish him God's blessing and he wishes to escort me.*

- *I hear beautiful melodies while I am being driven in a large car over a steep, paved hill. A great force hoists the car and it lands gently far beyond the brow of the hill.*

- *I am going up a tall hill very quickly, while carrying a car on my shoulder. I go over the hill which feels like a very steep climb with trees around.*

- *I am standing in an open space with a spectacular view of nature: blue sky, green pastures, and mountains. I wish I could fly.*

- *I am sitting in an airplane in flight.*

In the group *Driving, Climbing, Flying,* the first dream was very striking in Ada's mind because long after the fact, she realized that the dream occurred when she was having difficulty resolving the best method of organizing an academic book she was writing in a way that would be appealing to students. The guide who led her up the stairway turned out, in reality, to be a professor in the University of Vermont, who provided a significant reference as well as a related book he authored. By doing so, he certainly led her up a "stairway" to a "gorgeous scenery," which can be interpreted as the acceptance for publication, the valuable asset it was to the promotion process, and sharing with appreciative colleagues at conferences.

After receiving a copy she sent him, the professor wrote Ada a letter lauding the creativity of the text.

In the other dreams, other interesting symbols such as driving a car, being driven and hoisted over a hill referred to advancement, going somewhere, or overcoming a challenge. Peace and soaring of spirit were implied in the nature scene and flying in an airplane. However, only later would Ada appreciate their predictive value and the undercurrent of activities of invisible forces working on her behalf.

After waking from the following dreams, Ada again would feel transported particularly because they reflect so much of nature's most delightful features: stars, water from a rock, walking through flowing water, savoring coconut water – all of which filled her with joy that was shortlived.

Looking Skyward

- *In the night, I am lying on my back in the middle of a street. The sky is filled with bright stars and there is a half moon.*

Water: Fish, Lake, Running Stream

- *A large fish is dancing in the air. I catch it, massage its breast, then send it away with the agreement that it will return.*
- *I am sitting on a stone in a running stream. I call someone to drink from the beautiful, clear water under an overhanging rock. At another point I escape a harmless scorpion.*
- *I am walking abreast with a group of people through flowing water.*
- *Someone gives me a container filled with delicious coconut water. I drink it.*

The Crucible

No journey or achievement is without its challenges. At this stage, a backward look along the deep and winding pathways of the dig revealed to Ada that her teaching career and the long promotion process occurred as a crucible through which she was being given many lessons reflecting a significant and crucial segment of her soul journey.

Despite her many "imperfections," her dedication, enthusiasm, and innovative spirit to give her best never waned. She is now convinced that whatever her shortcomings might have been, they were meant to be instruments cutting away those parts of herself which were not in service to her spiritual advancement. Perhaps there was too much false pride in work, zeal for achievement, and emphasis on intellectual pursuits which developed into blinding ego attachments. In short, despite meditating, listening to, and reading literature of spiritual teachers, limited attention was being devoted to the real study and understanding of who she was spiritually becoming, a phase of her being that was crying out for attention through various symptoms. Ada was gradually being led to give attention to those areas that were out of sync with her "authentic sense of self." Ada now believes that the following dreams represented her inner chaos:

Wounds, Threatening Creatures, Danger

- *Rocks, small and big are being thrown in my direction but I am out of harm's way.*
- *I am running because I am being chased towards a dead end in a building. A small creature under a curtain bares its fangs, catches my hand, but I manage to escape.*

- ***I am with people around a table. A male sitting next to me strikes my upper right arm with a sharp pointed object and I begin to bleed. Bonnie, dressed in white, stands nearby.***
- ***About eight creatures like small rats are fighting and trying to get at my heel. A woman comes, leads me up a narrow path through an opening which leads to an upper landing where there is a meadow with flowers and a peaceful space.***

Despite all her efforts, it also appeared were obstacles and objections to her worthiness to be a successful candidate. This seemed to be reflected in the last theme, *Wounds, Threatening Creatures, Danger,* as in rocks "thrown in my direction," or being wounded with "a sharp pointed object," and rats "fighting and trying to get at my heel." But Ada seemed to be "out of harm's way," as she "manages to escape," guarded by Bonnie, a spirit guide, who rescued her by leading her to an" upper landing" where there were "flowers and a peaceful space" indicating support and final triumph.

However, despite the obstacles and objections, in the Spring of 1997, Ada finally received the news that by a majority vote, she was granted the position on the "upper landing," the coveted promotion to full professor. The dreams of flowing streams, clear water, and bright stars indicated this positive outcome and feeling of tranquility. Of course, she also had a feeling of relief that a tedious phase in her career had successfully ended and she was filled with gratitude mixed with a sense of mystery.

Ada's awareness of the generous support from several individuals has increased tremendously during the course of current reflections on her dreams. She now also regards with respect those who may have planted obstacles, and inserted harm and negativity; they were her teachers on so many levels, giving lessons on her soul journey. Again, what was really important here? A victory? A cause to have a "better than" mentality? A reason to rejoice for getting ahead ? Glad as she was that the process was finally over, Ada knew too well how distant those thoughts were from her deepest feelings.

Ada sensed that the promotion was for her a process reaching far beyond the external events. There was a silent, perplexing, inner journey being played out and mysteriously guided through dreams. The total journey was a crucible for unusual experiences, challenges, interactions, all part of a broader scheme registered in the psyche, and to be slowly comprehended only through a continuing process of introspection.

Even while being spiritually nourished, Ada's distance from her true sense of self corresponded with the emotional distance she found herself cultivating towards some co-workers whom, as previously stated, she can now truly regard with greater clarity and gratitude as among her best teachers. Through them she was often spurred to question her dreams as she continued to excavate more diligently, to view herself through new lens while the digging continued with new fervor only to be faced later with an illusion.

CHAPTER TWELVE

Becoming liberated from the bondage of negativity... lets you realize your tremendous value as a person...achieving emotional freedom gives you ongoing access to your own power center during jubilant times and in adversity. Orloff [1]

The dreamer may want to change attitudes, mind-sets, emotional reactions and behaviors implied in the dream...By understanding themselves and putting that understanding into action, they live more authentic, productive, and rewarding lives. Barrick[2]

AN ILLUSION

I t was with much marvel and deep humility that as Ada reflected more intensely on the relationship between her dreams and her professional activities, it became more clear that she was unaware of the integral role of the dreams in the intriguing interplay between her professional and spiritual life. It is interesting, Ada discovered, that she can frequently go to church, read the Bible and works of spiritual teachers, believe them, and still ignorant of who she really is. In the inner exploration of the *What* and *When* into her subconscious, Ada realized she was further undergoing a subtle and deep transformation which could eventually explain the *WHY*. She must be patient, as it was in the continuing process of the journey, not any particular destination, that the obscure *Why* would begin to be revealed.

Long, tedious activities had culminated in the achievement of a professional goal which Ada thought would have been the prime signal of her "blooming," but it turned out that was only a recapitulating station on the journey. Under the circumstances, Ada should have celebrated what could be regarded as a "victory" by ringing bells, or throw a huge outrageous party complete with colorful decorations, dancing, music, beating drums, and celebratory fireworks. But that was far removed from the feeling she could recall. After gratefully dining with a small group of friends, Ada became strangely conscious of a lack of something, a haunting desire for a deeper knowing, leading her perhaps to something non-academic, non-intellectual, outside the mundane professional world. The search for "something more" which began decades before was still not satisfied, was still relentless, and continued its nagging sensation with intensity.

There was something far more mysterious, tantalizing, elusive, shrouded, and precious - the continuing heart-tug search for the yet-to-be-discovered "something more." It was a spiritual hunger which still yearned to be sated. How many years had it been since the experience at the patch of begonia where she declared "That's how I should be blooming?" The memory kept spurring the need for further digging to find the *Why* of her dreams which may hold the secret and the clue to the blooming whatever that is! Apparently, it had yet to occur! Breathnach expressed very well, that as a spiritual hunger, "something more" is not a want, but a need felt missing from within. Ada became aware that her blooming was deeply connected to her spirituality in ways beyond her current awareness.

What is spirituality? After asserting, "no one can dictate your spiritual identity for you," Orloff describes spirituality as "a viscerally experienced energy that opens your heart enabling you to feel a higher power. It has nothing to do with intellectualizing, expectations, politics, or social norms. You are the only one who will know if your connection is viable."[3] For Ada, that definition could not be more accurately expressed. She was led to believe that the need to satisfy the spiritual hunger was in part foreshadowed through her previously mentioned dream where she was led by Mom to a new vista, a lighted doorway, a place of illumination. According to some dream authors, light indicates wisdom or enlightenment. Was that leading her to find what was missing? Could it be the doorway lighting her path to true self-discovery, her blooming?

> *Mom is standing by an open door and she smilingly invites me to go in. The place is filled with light. We walk briefly together, but I see nothing, then I am alone.*

Repeated dreams of biking over a hill, climbing a perpendicular wall, or car being hoisted, or carrying a car on her shoulder, taking an elevator, or hearing music, and playing with children would seem to indicate success in achieving her professional goal, but there may be other meanings yet to be revealed. Cayce explained that significant meanings occur in dreams on several levels at once and Kaplan also agrees that dreaming itself comes in different stages and levels. In addition, the dreamer plays an important role in the dream interpretation due to intimacy with related life circumstances.

When one is too close to a painting, attention is likely to be focused on small, isolated, close details. Standing from a distance reveals a more comprehensive perspective. Similarly, Ada realized that her "climbing" was an effort that went far beyond her career, but where was it going? Where was the door that Mom opened leading? What is still missing? How can it be recognized? She sometimes felt lost in the current exploration; the map showing the path to a professional goal once seemingly buttressed by spiritual practice was leading to somewhere else far beyond any experience up to that time. Evidently, the silent, uncertain, internal digging and climbing must continue. She may be alone in her quest, but not without assistance for which her gratitude cannot be measured. What other discoveries could be ahead?

CHAPTER THIRTEEN

The journey to self-knowledge is an exhilarating, yet humbling one. As it unfolds keep distilling the core message of Emotional Freedom: outer events may be the stimulus for an upset, but how you choose to respond determines your experience. Openness to such growth is more important than intellectual knowing. Orloff [1]

Our attitudes and emotions clearly reflect our state of being. They offer not only ways of reviewing growth patterns, but also a way of measuring thoughts, words, and actions in the light of universal laws, thus enabling us to produce a more creative, spiritually focused life experience. Furst.[2]

A NEW SHIFT IN SELF-KNOWLEDGE

Experiences that Ada could count on from time to time for solace, strength, and rejuvenation, were her encounters with many special individuals, and spiritual group meetings.

All along her life's journey into maturity, it seemed special people had been placed in Ada's way to give her support and direction. Their personalities were like beacons of hope and confidence in the rough stages of her journey, and to them Ada will always be profoundly grateful for the honor of meeting them on her path: teachers, mentors, professionals, friends, strangers, mystics, and spiritual guides.

At special meetings, whether they took the form of lectures given by a renowned leader, such as the Dalai Lama in Central Park or Benjamin Crème's return to Manhattan, a gathering of Sai Baba devotees, a shaman guide on a trip to the Machu Picchu Temple of the Incas high in the Andes, or a Peace Conference in the Netherlands, Ada returned nourished, somewhat more balanced. After each elevating experience, she was reminded of the similar uplifting and internal change she felt after her sabbatical trip to Mexico.

Ada was convinced that the repeated climbing in her dreams was the symbol which referred to the achievement of her promotion. That was an illusion. On the one hand, it appeared as a reality, but on the other, it was but a milestone far removed from the real blooming signaled years before by the begonia blossoms. Dreams of climbing hills and stairs, getting into elevators, uphill biking and driving never stopped; they simply continued more frequently.

Following her promotion, any uplifting experience was soon forgotten. It was as though Ada was functioning on one level in her day-to-day activities, while on another, she was being guided by an unknown mysterious inner management system.

The interplay which she believed was previously between her professional career and her spiritual life was now shifting to a new focus at another level: the need for alignment of her spiritual growth with her emotional well-being was taking center stage, becoming more pronounced, and being reflected through interpersonal interactions some of which were wounding. She had depended too much on external sources for what she thought gave her emotional stability. Something was missing and the time had come to look within herself with deepest scrutiny!

Commenting on the journey to self-knowledge, Orloff mentions that openness to growth in emotional freedom is more important than mere intellectual knowing. Ada realized that going beyond her superficial knowledge of psychology and religious rites and ceremonies turned out to be the ultimate plunge to a region of herself which she had neglected and taken for granted. Apparently, it was now highly important to become more intimate with this aspect of herself. The dig became more daunting and the example of the otter gave pause for reflection.

CHAPTER FOURTEEN

Just as the otter needs to dive deep to get to the ocean floor; similarly, we need to get underneath symptoms of any disharmony...our descent to the bottom of our issues help us purge any attachments to patterns of past behavior...sometimes delving is scary. Guerrero[1]

PATHWAYS TO EXPERIENCES
BEYOND THE DOORWAY

In 1998, Ada was guided to enroll in a Graduate Studies program focusing on Feminine Texts in Literature and Women's History in the antebellum south of the United States. Was this the doorway and the vista that Mom showed and walked through with Ada? She was not sure, but it was through this new in-depth program that her eyes were opened in a different way, to the powerful energy of women's emotions, and the dynamic ways in which those emotions were channeled for good or ill. Ada was forced to mindfully examine her own emotions to understand how they were functioning within herself, especially in her relationships.

Previous to that point, that was not an important matter for examination. Ada just went along with the flow of her life acting and achieving as she thought she was being directed intuitively. Her goals were accomplished in accordance with "outside criteria" but to the neglect of internal emotional dynamics for balance and soul health. She considered herself as one who was friendly, and expressed love for others, except those who assaulted her, thus establishing the need for her protective shield, emotional distancing.

However, the dreamer was undergoing another change. It was as though Ada entered a new dimension, exploring unfamiliar terrain, but equipped with new lenses, digging to identify and more clearly understand her full range of emotions. How intimate was she with them? Did she ever honestly own her emotions? To what feelings were they linked? Was she controlling them or were they controlling her, harming or protecting her? By being unaware of their impact on her being, was she contributing to negativity towards others? Was she really aware of the effect of others' emotions on her own well-being? To what extent were her emotional responses to negativity retarding or enhancing her spiritual health and advancement? By focusing on outer events, was she neglecting the power of her emotions to her disadvantage? How did she express them? Are there emotions she was denying or unaware of? The digging at this point, became more daring, adventuresome, a frightening, personal and crucial responsibility. The "self-training" program was well underway. With the flood of such questions, she felt as though she were still a stranger to herself! This was comparable to having in her own home, a room of treasures which she locked away, disregarded, and hid the key!

Before arriving in the United States, she felt much confidence in herself but that confidence she realized was rooted in education, social conditioning, and mundane meanings or understanding of "success." What seemed important was others' approval and perception of her as "nice," and "good teacher," and "successful"; or whether her actions pleased or impressed others, even some which she may have carried out with suppressed resentment. Comments such as "informative presentation" and "good speaker," gave a passing ego boost, but insults or behaviors of negativity from others, on the other hand, were bruising and debilitating to her sense of self, a disconnect from the confident, outgoing person she once thought herself to be.

In retrospect, Ada was far from knowing how disconnected she was from what Sara Breathnach and others refer to as "the authentic self," which we search for fruitlessly in outside sources. What that would mean for Ada personally, was the next level of her consciousness through intimate connection with her emotions. Her dreams would lead her as a result of experiences which would prepare her for the shift and a new level of newness from within. "When the student is ready, the teacher appears," is a truism which must not be ignored. In a dream, Mom had ushered her through a lighted doorway. What was beyond it? It seemed so many experiences had prepared Ada for this new phase, yet the ones that lay ahead beyond the doorway, as in the dream, were pending and would be illuminating.

Ada was about to have some bitter-sweet experiences on a long road ahead. For one thing, she was unaware of her many fears, which Gary Zukav refers to as "frightened parts of the personality." There were variations of fear in her personality which her dreams were about to reveal through unexpected avenues.

CHAPTER FIFTEEN

...we are subjected only to those experiences necessary to spiritual growth. This perhaps explains why even the seemingly good suffer... for suffering often releases spiritual powers that aid others. Also, it teaches compassion through understanding and gives us greater patience accompanied by an appreciation of life in general. Sechrist[1].

The dream also serves to spotlight an aspect of our life that we are overlooking, neglecting or mishandling...when we pay attention to the emotional content of our dreams, we have the opportunity to resolve our deeper feelings and recover more quickly from life's emotional crises. Barrick[2].

ENDEAVORS, HIDDEN TREASURES, AND DREAMS

Two Projects

During 1999 and 2000, one outgrowth of the Women's Studies Program was that Ada was being drawn into finding creative ways to engage her students in exploring the scope of historical events over the last millennium in one exhibit, and in a second, illustrate the vast and vital contributions of women spanning several areas of endeavor, including literature, journalism, the civil rights and women's rights movements. Several activities were organized to involve various groups of students over a two-semester period, a daring approach beyond many traditional methods of engaging students. While it became a rewarding and fulfilling process, Ada did not anticipate how time-consuming and exhausting it would be, as one interesting activity opened the possibility for another resulting in two exhibits instead of just one that was originally planned.

Gary Zukav, in *Heart of the Soul,* explains that one way we avoid painful emotions is to escape into activity. This may be true, but not so in this instance. As difficult as the activities were, Ada became aware that they were inspired for some purpose and expression unknown to her at that time. She felt as though she was being carried along by something she was unable to resist, and had she ignored the urge, Ada knew she would have regretted that call to action regardless of personal cost. The first exhibit spanned humanity's progress of invention, revolutions, and setbacks of wars of man's own making. The second, the Women's Exhibit was particularly poignant as Ada became more sensitive than usual, not only to the vast contributions of women, but also to the oppression which many endured over the millennium.

Several political, social, and economic situations rendered them vulnerable and powerless, yet many triumphed over adversity. Embedded in these women's lives were wide-ranging emotional implications. How did they cope and make breakthroughs overcoming barriers? Was it with anger, retaliation, bullying, revenge, unresolved confrontations, false accusations and humiliations, destructive criticisms that they endured, or did they use proactive measures? For many who triumphed, they utilized transforming approaches with tenacity, determination coupled with skillful strategies. They broke down barriers through activism, such as, writing, sports, journalism, or political involvement for justice, etc. Ada felt an eager openness to deepened knowledge of some outstanding tide-changing women: Harriet Tubman, Golda Meir, Margaret Thatcher, Rosa Parks, Sui Kyi Aung Sang, Barbara Walters, Oprah Winfrey, and several others. Students were made aware of the latent genius of these women.

The criticisms and compliments regarding both projects were received by Ada with calm and gratitude as belonging to the force which directed them. Harmon Bro maintains that Cayce describes a higher realm of the subconscious which provides patterns of guidance which "are in effect the creative currents of the divine itself, moving through human affairs like some great unseen Gulf Stream.[3] Ada strongly believes that these creative currents flowed through the lives of these women, and what she felt in that silent space of her being, as an unusual thrill, may have been just the minutest microcosm of those currents, but she knew they were beyond her.

In the dig of *What* and *When* of her dreams towards finding the *Why*, the outcome of those projects was remarkable. Ada realized that in the process of organizing them there was a priceless, unique emotional experience she had not recognized before.

Some people choose to end their careers with much fanfare celebrating an earned milestone, and rightfully so. Comparatively, it could well be stated that staging exhibits was an insignificant event. For Ada, the two exhibits, simply organized with her students' involvement brought her career to a satisfying, invaluable culmination. For her, it was a unique gift to all who helped and showed interest; it was a retrospective celebration of human life with all its triumphs and adversities over the last millennium, a tribute to all members of the college community, to those who contributed to Ada's progress, but also, an expression of gratitude to the "creative currents of the divine" which guided Ada all along since 1976 when she first set foot in a strange new city, and a different culture which became a crucible, changing the trajectory of her life.

While working on the exhibits, the period Fall 1999 to Spring 2000 was no less rich with dreams, and Ada still continues to ponder some of their meanings to this day. Still clothed in the metaphoric language of the subconscious, what really were their exact messages? As Barrick suggests, "paying attention to the emotional content of our dreams," has advantages, such as "resolving deeper feelings" and recovering from "emotional crises." Do the dreams in Series O reveal anything about Ada's emotions?

Dreams During Fall 1999 – Spring 2000 – SERIES O

Being Chased:

- *I am being chased for a long time by a male. I finally elude him.*
- *I have a diamond and I am being pursued along a zigzag track. I am afraid but always ahead and aware of my attacker. I finally elude him and reach home safely.*

There was no question. She was again being chased and she eluded her pursuers! But was she running from someone or avoiding something within herself? In the second chase dream, she held something precious, a diamond, which she is protecting from her attacker whom she evades. Ada now believes that she was being chased by the varying emotions she felt during the course of the exhibits, while at the same time she recognized the potential for learning for the students, and the release of creativity and new energy that was engendered.

Climbing:

- *I climb the hill and enter a room where Mom is lying on a bed. She gives me a kiss on my mouth, looks happy, but while lying on her stomach, she slides away in the opposite direction. I am filled with love for her and I begin to cry very hard.*
- *It is a high hill. I find myself standing and looking at an incredible view in the distance far away. A grey, blue mountain stretches far on both sides of the hill. Immediately before me are two little boys, sitting, leaned back, smiling at me in a mischievous way. The space surrounding me on the hill and the breathtaking view feel out of the ordinary.*

Ada was still reaching for "something more" and Mom's affectionate kiss during her visit seemed to bring a boost, a solace and assurance of love in the struggle. The second dream of a blue mountain in a distant scene with a "breathtaking view" indicated a space of elevation from within that Ada had yet to really feel within her grasp. Yet on that high hill, she was being invited to be the carefree, happy spirit of two little boys. Children do teach Ada so frequently, in her dreams as well as in everyday circumstances.

Flowers and Dew:

- *Children are playing while hitched to each other, sliding down hills and laughing. Then I am in an open meadow where the grass is green, lush and heavy with dew. I am tempted to wash my face with the dew but I am attracted to a patch of heavily clustered white flowers which grow barely off the ground. I pick a cluster and hold it admiringly in my hand.*
- *Trees are losing their blossoms in the wind. The ground is carpeted with the pink blossoms and I hold out my hands while laughing and trying to catch those in the air as they are being blown in my direction.*

Again, the symbols of happy children and flowers recurred during the course of working on the projects. Flowers epitomize beauty and transition into newness and growth. Ada holds a cluster of white flowers and admires them; in the second dream she is walking on a carpet of pink blossoms, and as if at childlike play, she tries to catch blossoms being blown in her direction. While the immediate relevance to the exhibits was not clear, the two dreams were reflective of something that would bring joy. The predictive quality was reinforced by the following dreams:

House, Buildings

- *I am busy with a broom sweeping a large area of a house*
- *The building looks like a church. On the pavement outside, some old furniture is waiting to be cleared away. Inside, people are lining the walls with white material, very white; some parts are trimmed with white lace.*

Ada believes that the house represents her being, and the sweeping is her intent to become more informed about her emotional self as deeply as possible, and by sweeping, she was clearing out that which is inhibiting. Old furniture to be disposed of repeats the message of discarding negative emotions that are obstacles to her spiritual growth. Continuing the predictive pattern, dreams of keys, milk and beverage provided further clues to what may be ahead in the dig.

Keys

- *I am in a building where I seem to be given a new position, to be in charge of a school or something. I feel reluctance. I ask for the keys and I am given a cloth bag, bigger than my fist, filled with keys.*
- *I hold a key and put it in the door.*

Milk, Beverage:

- *I see three bottles of rich white milk. I drink nearly all of it and I am feeling guilty.*
- *I am aware of three medium glasses of rich milk. One is presented to me, but I did not drink it.*
- *Is it a park? I drink two cans of delicious coconut water; I then seem to be in a church environment where there is a glass case of figurines.*

Ada believes that keys were given to her to open more doors leading her to "something more," the *Why*. "I hold a key and put it into a door" seems to denote access or opportunity to be experienced. As if to give further credence and reinforcement to the keys to open doors or opportunities, or what lies ahead regarding her advancement in self-knowledge, she drinks milk and coconut water, both liquids for nourishment and sustenance, symbolic of the nourishment to be received later.

Although the theme of music has already been addressed, at this period of intense working with students on the exhibits, dreams of music are repeated many times. Singing, harmonies, instrumental music, even Ada's Dad is engaged in the atmosphere of peace and joy which also characterizes the following dreams. Ada is conducting a combined children's choir, but in one dream she was to play a hymn on the organ but did not have the music, indicating a lack of preparation for whatever is imminent. It seems more time is necessary for her to be receptive to what the future holds.

Music:

- *I am strongly aware of my friend, Randy's presence. Then afterwards I face an unusual panoramic view of beautiful colors and musical harmonies filling the air.*
- *I am among young, white, happy teen-age girls singing happy songs. One is playing the organ. I am supposed to be doing something but the action is fuzzy.*
- *I hear beautiful singing. Dad is singing, but his back is turned towards me, so I tap him on the shoulder. He turns around and is pleased to see me.* **(On awakening, I tell him thanks for the visit.)**
- *All seem ready. There is an atmosphere of joy. I sit at the organ and attempt to play the hymn, but I did not have the music.*
- *I am directing two combined children's choirs. Between me and the children is a huge* area *of various gorgeous flowers. What a great feeling after I wake up!*

Water:

> • *I can't remember exactly where I am, but I am aware of seeing very clear water, even white sand at the bottom. I even dip my finger in it!*

However, Ada believes positive energies were at work within her. She was given the keys and the nourishment necessary to continue her quest. A further confirmation is given by clear water and" white sand at the bottom," so soothing and emotionally inviting that she even dips her finger in it, as if irresistibly trying to touch, feel, experience, and indulge in the beauty and richness of what she sees.

Several times Ada has read through these dreams which occurred during and after her work on the exhibits. The process of working with students was at once a creative expression and an emotional release of anger, frustration, shock, and resentment. In trying to interpret the dreams, Ada was unable to see the compatibility between her then uncomfortable emotional issues and the above positive dreams. Her inner emotional state did not appear to be in harmony with them. This could possibly explain Orloff's statement that "dreams tap a creative universe that dwarfs logic, materializing options from the void."[4] It became clear to Ada that she needed more clarity in understanding the world of her emotions. She remembered questioning herself, "What steps do I need to take to be assured of living my best life now?" "Who am I becoming?" "How can I emotionally experience my optimal best in this life?" Apparently, there is much for Ada to learn during this dig of *What* and *When* to understand the *Why* of her dreams, and clarity regarding her emotions is vitally important among the clues!

CHAPTER SIXTEEN

Your emotions are the best of friends...They continually bring to your attention what you need to know...Without that knowledge you cannot change. Zukav[1].

The world confronts us with countless challenges and predicaments that arouse the energies of our emotions. If we can direct those energies to a positive end...we are transmuting our emotions. Bennett-Goleman[2].

A LECTURE AND SPOTLIGHT ON EMOTIONS

Emotions as friends? Transmuting emotions? What evocative concepts! As already mentioned, during the year long process, in a deep, tranquil silence and solitude, known only to herself, through the medium of the Women's Studies Program and the student activities it generated, Ada's emotional infrastructure came under much self-scrutiny.

Shortly after the completion of the exhibits, she had the opportunity of listening to a lecture by Dr. Orloff, an intuitive energy psychiatrist, whose lecture on positive energy, its relationship to emotions and dreams made an indelible impact on Ada. Orloff was a key, and her message a door! Although not entirely new, her message had a fresh and penetrating appeal! Seated as a stranger among members of a large audience, Ada could not help feeling that Dr. Orloff's message was meant specifically for her attention. Ada learnt two important issues applicable to her: First, how important it is to be aware of what the author refers to as "emotional vampires" who suck the energy of others through negative behaviors. Second, and more significant, Ada began to realize she bore some of the characteristics of an intuitive empath - one whose deep sensitivity absorbs surrounding energy; one who thrives where there is peace and harmony, and is debilitated by noise, conflict, and negativity, and suffers as a result!

An expanded version of Orloff's message in her books generated the spotlight for the continuing inner dig, revealing clues to Ada's long history of numbing fatigue in environments where there is insulting, loud, abusive language, harsh music, bullying or violent, abrasive, belittling behaviors.

In her former Social Work career, Ada recalled many such explosive displays and belittling outbursts which she found depressing in working with some clients. Yet, after many years, when she experienced similar instances whether from a stranger, professional, group participant, or minister, the impact took on a more stinging effect. Ada needed to answer for herself why she felt their effect so intensely? Evidently, she was not emotionally free, not immune to such energies, and hungered to be in a spiritual space comparable to that of the Buddha, an exemplar of emotional freedom! The Buddha's story will be explained later.

Dr. Orloff's lecture became a compelling call for Ada to consider her own negative response of aloofness as her protective shield against insults and demeaning criticisms. The lecturer's message explained for Ada why she felt charged with uplifting, revitalizing energy when she was in the presence of spiritual teachers, or even in the presence and stillness of sacred natural surroundings, such as, the colorful beauty of trees, flowers, rainbows, water, birds, and animals. She was outside the zone of negativity, and she was absorbing sublime manifestations of divinity.

The work on the exhibits gave her the inner readiness she needed to grasp Dr. Orloff's message more fully. Where previously it would have passed through one ear and out the other as having no relevance to her life due to her focused attention on outer issues, the lecture was an emotional wake-up call, which afforded a thorough examination from within. Receiving the message and realizing its impact was one thing, but locating the hidden areas of her embedded harmful response patterns within herself and changing them was quite another.

The cleansing required for changing her long unwitting practice of emotional distancing for protection became the next level for further self-study and self-awareness. Dr. Orloff's reference to "emotional freedom," struck a chord, stimulated Ada's curiosity, and she was determined to find out more about this tantalizing factor and its importance to her spiritual health.

CHAPTER SEVENTEEN

You cannot always change people or circumstances but you can always change the way energy is processed in your energy system. You only have to know where and how energy is being processed, and that is what emotions will tell you...When you ignore your emotions, you ignore that information. Zukav[1]

The more you cleanse your system of lies, errors, misunderstandings, energy blocks, emotional hang-ups, and desperation, the more cleanly you will enter the dream space. Kaplan[2]

EMOTIONAL FREEDOM
AS SELF-KNOWLEDGE

During this later stage of the dig, Ada became cognizant of two important issues. One was that by her aloofness, or refusing to be friendly to those whom she believed "offended her unjustly", was in reality, not the protective shield she firmly believed it to be; rather, it served to invite more abuse because, as she later learned, hers was also a negative energy attaching to, or magnetizing another negative energy! But the second and worse impact, Ada later realized, was the diminishing effect it had on her own spiritual self. In other words, under the guise of self-protection while absorbing negativity, she was allowing her capacity for expressing love to be weakened and diminished by assaults from others. Inadvertently, and in ignorance, she was returning what she received!! Why, because she was not emotionally conscious, not emotionally free! Is this possible? If so, how does one really become emotionally free?

In her eye-opening book on *Emotional Freedom,* Dr. Orloff provides a brilliant insight by stating that your value as a person is realized when you become liberated from the bondage of negativity. Isn't that a Buddha consciousness? How then does one become entirely liberated from or even become immune to the effects of negativity, outside one's self as well as from within?

While noting that it requires time and dedication to acquire such a state, thus gaining access to one's power center in good and bad times, Orloff further comments that "being free means surviving rejection, major and minor, without turning on yourself or allowing them to define you."[3] For Ada, this was an excellent change of perspective, but was easier said than done! That would be a quantum leap for Ada whose sense of self, to a great measure, was intimately related to external circumstances, such as her reputation and personal achievements. Where does one find one's power center? "Know thyself," said Socrates. "Study self, study self," Cayce repeated. It was as though these sayings were giving the key to understand what Jesus had previously said, "the kingdom of heaven is within," an abstraction that was too dense for Ada to comprehend. She was to realize later that studying self was a means of finding that heaven and that power center!

A frequent statement from Dad during Ada's young years was, "if you know better, do better!" Knowing better, she came to realize, is a continuing, transforming process occurring in many ways at different levels of self-study. More memorable were sayings from her mother who had often cautioned against retaliation. Like her Mom, the idea of "an eye for an eye and a tooth for a tooth," Ada had endorsed as self-destructive, but by also applying Mom's other precept "a soft answer turneth away wrath," she was aware that she evoked disdain from some emotional life force leechers. That approach was not in accordance with their practice of abusive behavior and false image of power. In addition, applications of assertiveness, as another strategy, done with the aggression that Ada had often observed, did not find a comfortable space in Ada's repertoire of defense methods.

Coinciding with her focus on emotional freedom, Ada was introduced to the work of Masuru Emoto, a Japanese scientist and researcher who had done extensive work on the crystal composition of water! Specifically, Emoto discovered that when exposed to negative language, the crystals in water were dark, blurry, and shapeless. In contrast, in an environment where positive words were spoken, the crystals in water were clear with beautiful, well defined shapes. How fascinating! If that were the case with visible water, how do cells in the human body appear where negativity dwells? Conversely, they must be beautifully defined in a biological environment nourished by positive words and attitudes!

Ada realized that her well-ingrained practice of aloofness and resentment against negative attackers was a mind-set that she had to change both for her offenders, as well as for her emotional and spiritual well-being. Although historically, her strategy may have "successfully protected" her from some people in her school years, in shared living quarters or work environments, she became convinced that her shield of protection was self-sabotaging, not physically or spiritually beneficial for her, nor did it recognize the good and the divine in the offender! This could be one answer for the persistence of conflicts and wars over the centuries. We have forgotten who we are as one writer puts it, "spiritual beings having a human experience," and not "human beings having a spiritual experience." We have departed from our initial spiritual purity by our choice to follow the promptings of the ego, or false self. Conflicts, destructive competition, bloody wars, oppression and varied forms of abuse have resulted over centuries. Ada realized that her negative energies were contributing to that ongoing global maelstrom.

Cayce emphasizes that studying self is not a short-term exercise. It is also Barrick's view that it is through dreams that we do "our emotional homework." Orloff confirms that to "conquer all emotions that impede freedom," dreams with their "encyclopedic vision" can lead us to what is" good and beautiful." Ada realized that as a heroine digging through *What* and *When* of her dreams, she must pursue diligently her emotional impediments in order to experience the good and beautiful linked to her desired emotional freedom and the *Why*.

Ada thought, "Mom, you did open a door and you let me in; I did not grasp your message; I was supposed to follow the light and find out what is beyond it, right?" Does the solution lie far ahead? It seemed Ada was being led by the light to new dimensions of self-understanding, mind expansion, and awakening to new truths as stimulants of emotional freedom!

What dreams did she have during this period that may reveal even a few hidden clues for the study and greater understanding of her emotional self? Did the dreams during the final months of Ada's career have a prophetic significance?

CHAPTER EIGHTEEN

All of our unresolved problems show up first in our dreams. Tanner.[1]

Your emotions are signposts that point to parts of yourself that require healing... Ignorance of your emotions results in being controlled by parts of yourself that are generating your emotions. Zukav.[2]

DREAMS – A CAREER ENDS AS THE MILLENNIUM CLOSES

During the Fall of the year 2000, Ada felt an inner urge to announce her retirement. Her announcement in early December brought an uncanny sense of relief, and she was convinced that her decision was right. Little did she know that she was being prepared to enter a new phase of emotional self-knowledge and without the slightest idea of the form it would take. Did she not dream about being given a bag of keys, and in another dream had put one in a door? On another level of meaning, the key she had put in the door was her decision for retirement.

She knew she was interested in Peace Work and trusted "the currents" to take her where she should be. Since it did not occur already, is it by doing Peace Work that the blooming would occur? How will it feel? Ada had often questioned herself. Before coming to New York, she had uttered from an unknown source within herself that she wanted to be like the abundantly flowering begonia blossoms that once caught her attention on the way to school. It seemed the *Why* of her dreams, her Emotional Freedom and her blooming were now interconnected, but finding the *why* remained a daunting issue, so the digging must go on.

Cayce emphasized the wisdom of studying one's body of dreams to recognize underlying patterns. During the final months of teaching service, Ada had several dreams, some of which are stated below:

Dreams during Fall 2000 - SERIES P

Rain

- *I am standing with some people who suddenly divided to stand on both sides of a grassy path. A heavy but gentle rain falls on them but I am not getting wet. Then from the distance beyond, a figure begins to form and quickly emerges as a woman in pink, with a crown on her head coming towards me. I think she is Mary, Jesus' Mother. She gives the back of her hand for me to kiss, then she faces the crowd. By this time there is no rain; she turns to me and smilingly says, "Ada, speak to the people." She vanishes; at that moment, I do not know what to say, but I think that once I open my mouth the words would come. I did not speak.*

Rain is a cleansing and healing symbol, but it is not falling on Ada. Those on whom the rain falls prepare a pathway for a spiritual figure, Mary, to deliver a message to Ada about what she is to do. She is about to retire, to whom then would she speak? Mary represents peace and purity of heart, qualities which Ada should aim to acquire and express in the next phase of her life.

Light

- *There is a fast moving object going towards the distant end of a long tunnel where there is a light. At the center of the tunnel, the object looks more like a yellow rose which comes back toward me with great speed, but by the time it reaches me it resembles a white dove which flies above me.*

Quite interesting is that in this dream, in a background of light, illumination, a yellow rose, a symbol of fullness and beauty returns to Ada as a dove, a symbol of peace, reinforcing Mary's presence of peace. It was later that Ada realized that the dream was related to her involvement with children in a Peace Program which will be further explained. What could dreams of an animal, a ball, and music have in common?

Animal

- *Is it a goat? Its nipples are large, swollen, and milk spews as the goat walks. I see a woman with a hungry child and recommend that she allows the child to suck the nipples.*

Ball

- *I have a ball about the size of a golf ball. I toss it in the air, very high but I do not see it fall!*
- *Someone throws a ball to me and I catch it!*

Music, Dancing, Laughter

- *I am bathing in a shallow bathtub with soapy water. As if moving it with a lever, someone unexpectedly raises me up, then gently lowers me again while I am laughing.*

- ***I am working with large groups of children*** (repeated in at least four dreams*), playing and singing. In the last dream, we are singing, "Joyful, joyful, we adore thee," while I play on the guitar.*

Without the slightest inkling of what would occur, all three dreams continued to give predictive messages about Ada's future activities with children as mentioned above. The Mediation/Peace Program was the goat with swollen nipples of milk which the children needed. The ball she threw, and one thrown back to her represented the exchanges with professionals regarding the offer of supervising the program which became for Ada, a kind of bath, a partial cleansing experience of her own emotions. "Someone unexpectedly raises me up...while I am laughing" referred to enjoyment in working with the children and compliments from staff members. Although at no time did she play the guitar with them or sing "Joyful, joyful we adore thee," Ada had engaged groups of the children in several peace songs. During that same period, two other dreams carried spiritual significance for Ada although she was unaware of any current relevance.

Honey

- *A shallow container of honey which I place on a table falls off. I am at the base of a concrete wall where it comes pouring down. I lick it up, as much as I can, and I also use my hands like a spatula to scoop up some of it.*

Church

- *I enter a beautiful brick church with a unique garden-like design inside. I follow a group of people as they leave through another gate.*

> *On my right, I can see a room with dazzling brightness which I wish to enter but didn't.*
> - *I am in a small chapel, and I am the last one in the line for receiving Holy Communion. I kneel and the priest gives me a cup of clear wine with many hosts. I swallow it all.*

If honey is, as has been said, the nectar of the gods, then it is something sweet, something to be relished, something nourishing, and Ada seems to be getting as much of it as she can. The meaning of this dream becomes more clear through the next two dreams with church as a spiritual symbol at their center. In the first is a garden design, a room dazzling with brightness; in the next, Ada drinks clear wine and hosts as she receives Holy Communion, additional symbols of spiritual essence or raised consciousness to be experienced in upcoming events. These dreams may have had a pleasing effect at the time Ada recorded them, but only later would their true meaning would be revealed. The last dream had greater clarity for Ada as she recorded it.

Difficulty/Fear/Attack (Last dream before leaving work in December)

> - *I am trying with much difficulty to untie a huge knot which seems like the heavy withes of trees locked into each other. While working at it, there are men groping at my breasts, lifting my skirt and looking under it. I have no pants on. I am scared; I call for help and I see a dark-skinned woman passing by.*

In this series, this "body of dreams," the last dream which occurred before leaving work in December 2000, was the only one which Ada believed she could interpret with any degree of certainty. Ada believed there were unfavorable, discrediting comments made against her. However, Ada had no regrets; her real tribute lay within her heart where it was expressed and shone glowingly with gratitude and appreciation for a career of dedicated, unstinting service, shortcomings and successes, forging and reshaping her while unconsciously evolving with an uncanny, quiet guidance to new realms of herself.

Her entanglement among the "withes of trees locked into each other," and the feeling of assault, her vulnerability of "no pants on," the cruel and insulting "groping and lifting of her skirt," reflected the negativity of the environment she was in. Why was Ada having difficulty untying "a huge knot?" Ada believes that the huge knot like the "heavy withes of trees locked into each other" referred to her own entangled emotions from which she was trying to break free. She felt shock and bitter resentment and more than she realized, Ada had absorbed their negative impact from others to her own detriment.

Paradoxically, in the body of dreams, Series A-N, what Ada found to be most baffling as a pattern, was that, coinciding with some of her most trying circumstances, her dreams seemed to provide opposite messages. As in the last Dream Series N, Ada's immediate work environment was challenging. Yet, her dreams had positive themes of rain, and a lady with a crown on her head, light in a tunnel changing to a rose then a dove, milk, catching a ball thrown to her, receiving communion, music and singing, and scooping up honey! Although she felt dubious as to their separate meanings, collectively, they seemed to be uplifting and different in message from the last dream where she tried to undo an entangled knot.

In December 2000, with contented, peaceful resignation, Ada knew intuitively that this service period in her life had come to a close. She retired and left her workplace as quietly as she had arrived twenty-one years earlier, giving gratitude to the Creator for a space and a place in time for her life which so far spanned benevolent encounters, enriching opportunities, experiences where adversity blended with countless blessings to provide lessons for self-knowledge and spiritual enrichment from a nurturing universe.

CHAPTER NINETEEN

Words impart energy that can be enlivening or malignant... Whether words set off a love bomb or a noxious explosion, they transfer energy to the target, eliciting a response. You can wield this force for construction or destruction. The aim is always to treat yourself and others well. Orloff [1].

...if the dreamer needs insight and understanding, it (the psyche) gives him lessons and even discourses. If he needs shaking up, it gives experiences - beautiful or horrendous...Bro [2]

A BLESSED EXPERIENCE

Working With Children

After her retirement, with mind-expanding knowledge provided by such fascinating authors as, Kaplan, Sechrist, Orloff, Zukav, Browne, Emoto, and others, Ada became a Mediator in a Public School after completing Marshall Rosenberg's training program in Non-Violent Communication. That activity seemed to reflect her previous dream of being given a bag of keys and putting one in the door! Working with the children became the opened door, the opportunity to serve the cause of Peace which Ada had long desired. It was as though the two years in that capacity fed her yearning to serve children, help them recognize the emotions behind their pain, to respond with peace, and use practical ways to release the pain they experience at home and school. It was a teaching and a learning experience for Ada.

Ada recalled one session with five girls whom the teacher described as "menacing trouble-makers, sneering and calling each other names" in her fifth grade class, and Ada was asked to intervene. In a private room, she arranged the stubborn, pouting, vicious girls in a circle and gave each a flower to silently study for some minutes. After some slow breathing exercises, then explaining the power of the breath, followed by Ada's several questions, each girl saw herself and the others as reflections of the flowers. They began to recognize each other's beauty which they expressed by voicing the good they admired. They could appeal to each other to return to the friendship they once knew from third grade; they realized that by their lies about each other and fighting they were hurting instead of appreciating each other's inner beauty. As the tears rolled down, the voices and words softened and became apologetic as anger was released. Ending with Whitney Houston's rendition of "The Greatest Love of All," Ada found that her technique of connecting the students with themselves through nature and music had a positive effect beyond her expectations. Because nature, children, and music frequently featured in Ada's dreams, they were often woven into the strategies she used to reach quite a few of the children with deep emotional pain.

On one occasion, visitors from Turkey who were interested in Peer Mediation Programs in the United States were impressed when they questioned the students regarding how they resolved their conflicts. They also commented on the children's rendition of peace songs as a special treat.

Previous to the arrival of the visitors, Ada had three interesting predictive dreams:

- *I am looking at vegetables I had planted in a garden. They look healthy, and a woman who is standing nearby admires them.*
- *Someone lifts me up high with one hand, walks with me hoisted past some people who are gathered for a meeting. Then the person walks me back again still hoisted. I am smiling and feeling light. One lady is also smiling.*
- *I look outside and see people marching. One carries a pole with a symbol at the top. I hear the word 'Peace' and believe my name is connected to it.*

Ada's interpretation was that the work she had done with the children was symbolized by the healthy vegetables; she was lifted up or felt elated by the positive impressions of the visitors, and the third dream seemed to endorse the peace work with the children. The above dreams appeared to be a continuation of others in which children were frequently singing, playing or hugging Ada or bringing her fruits.

Viewed from a broad spectrum of events, the challenging peace activities in which she engaged children and teachers could be compared to just one grain of sand on a vast seashore. For Ada, it bore her imprint as another episode in her life to which she was mysteriously led in the forward movement towards a deeper exploration of her own elusive emotional universe. It was a blessed assurance, a blessing in disguise.

CHAPTER TWENTY

You cannot grow spiritually without learning how to detach from your emotions and understand them as products of the way energy is processed in your energy system...Zukav [1]

...mindfulness can be emotionally freeing: it brings an active awareness to our otherwise automatic emotional patterns, interposing a reflecting consciousness between emotional impulse and action. And that breaks the chain of emotional habit. Bennett-Goleman [2]

INTERFACE OF THE EMOTIONAL AND SPIRITUAL SELF

Ada's spiritual progress and refinement had yet to undergo further rigorous purification of her emotional self to enhance, rather than retard her growth. Other unforeseen painful experiences would provide new lens through which she could view the level of emotional freedom she had yet to understand and perhaps attain someday. Her association with children sharpened her awareness where she became more mindful of her own deep feelings of empathy, gentleness and compassion, as well as seeing in a new way, the innate beauty which children have and can convey so naturally. What a different feeling from resentment and aloofness which were stumbling blocks in herself, occupying her cells, stealing and undermining her spiritual vigor!

At the time the events occurred, she was unaware of the significant extent to which her interactions with some adults would impact her in painfully advancing her progress. To them Ada now owes immense gratitude. She is aware that to some readers, this may seem so trivial and insignificant; it begs the question, "Why bother to mention them? That's nothing compared to traumas and permanent emotional wounds from relationships and life's battles that others have endured! Everybody encounters adversity at one time or another, sometimes for a major part of their lives: imprisonment, abandonment, loss and separation, betrayal, financial ruin, sudden and cruel death of a loved one, sustained physical and sexual abuse, calamities of nature, war injuries, etc. What do you have to complain about?" That may be so. However, depending on many factors, upbringing and cultural conditioning, for example, each person's reaction to life situations is different.

Where communication and relationships are concerned, it is not only the words or actions that can puncture one's emotional being, it is also the underlying intention, venom, and potency of negative energy by which they are fueled and fired that produces a wounding effect. In her Social Work career, Ada could recall several qualifying examples. There were men over forty years of age who still recalled the repeated humiliating and emotionally strangling criticisms of a father, and the unresolved repressed anger found its way into adulthood, then unconsciously expressed through abuse of an innocent, helpless wife or son. Understanding how emotions function as energy within one's being is as vital to spiritual retardation or growth as knowing which foods are detrimental or wholesome to one's physical health! This understanding is imperative for self-knowledge.

However, Ada was again intent on exploring more important questions, "Why does one feel such a wound of negative emotional energy from leechers?" Our world is a world of daily inevitable interactions with others. "Is it not possible to become immune to the impact of negative energy?" Ada began to realize that this is at the heart of emotional freedom linked with spiritual awareness, which was so well exemplified by the Buddha, a story soon to be discussed.

In studying and knowing self as a humbling experience, Orloff did explain that "outer events may be the stimulus for an upset, but how you choose to respond determines your experience. Such an experience can provide growth which transcends intellectual understanding."[3] Brilliant, Ada thought. Here is a deepened reason for studying herself! Blaming others for her negative feelings is completely missing the point!

Working with the children over several sessions enabled Ada to examine her own emotions by exploring and observing more deeply during silent moments, her own feelings as they are impacted by negative "outer events" from others. She needed to tap into those areas of her emotional self that had not been previously accessed or given adequate attention. Are there more weaknesses or strengths to be discovered? The adventure of the dig seems unending, but she is her own heroine, delving like the otter, to the deepest depths for clues, messages, and lessons from unexpected encounters.

CHAPTER TWENTY-ONE

The emotions you are working with will shape the synchronicities you experience... such auspicious intersections are bona fide intuitive moments when energetic forces align via synchronicities to assist you emotionally. Orloff [1]

Thoughts of revenge only bind us to the one who wounded us. They keep our pain alive...what we focus on grows.... So if we focus on the situation where we were hurt and injured we are continuing to give life and fuel to it. We must feed the thoughts and actions that empower our lives and starve those that harm us. Smith. [2]

Mastering emotional energy and grasping how you got there is as important as what you have attained. The process, always the process – synchronicities are part of that richness. Orloff. [3]

THREE TRANSFORMATIVE ENCOUNTERS

Three encounters in closely timed sequence, had a sharpening, illuminating effect on the link between the degree of Ada's emotional freedom and her level of spiritual awareness. Her feelings of protective aloofness and harbored resentment were reflective of the emotional aspects of herself that were claiming her intense and honest evaluation! Whereas previously, unaware that others were a mirror of her own negative emotions at this point, in her estimation, all three of these encounters challenged her to change her intellectual focus on "leechers," to studying closely what was happening within herself - her world of thoughts, her feelings, her own emotions, and her responses! Sechrist records Cayce as saying, "the thing that irritates you the most in others is found self! Else why would it bother you?"[4]. Now, that is a pathway to self-knowledge and authenticity, and Ada needed to wear a magnifying glass to thoroughly scrutinize this region within herself if she is to be free.

The first encounter relates to a social worker in the school where Ada worked. Ada had just completed an enjoyable session with some children and was ushering them through a main door when the social worker abruptly emerged from her enclosed space with hateful, flaring eyes and rage cursing at Ada, who after a few minutes of shock, asked the reason for such a performance towards her. The social worker responded that the client in her office was lying about her finances in order to receive more money from the government! "If that is so, why are you so angry with me?" Ada asked without rancor while she was seething within.

Without responding, the social worker abruptly walked away then slammed her door in Ada's face! Ada felt insulted, angry, and demeaned!

Much to her surprise, on two successive days, the social worker expressed apologies. Ada was later informed that at a recent Staff meeting, the social worker heard many favorable comments from teachers about Ada's intervention with the children in the Peer Mediation Program. Was there a connection? Was that why Ada was being targeted with anger? She was not sure, but Ada realized that she must be always be on the alert for sudden changes of behavior in relationships that previously enabled frequent friendly exchanges.

More importantly, such occurrences were checkpoints on her emotional status, one of the meaningful synchronicities! Was that meant for Ada to ask if she was lying to herself about how strong or fragile she was? Was she really aware of and in charge of her emotions? As Ada reminisced on her feelings, she held some resentment towards the social worker due to the undeserved insult, and wondered if the apologies came because she did not express her anger with equal viciousness or aloofness. What would have been the outcome if she had chosen to retaliate in like manner? Ada was certain that had she done so, she would have disliked herself miserably.

A second encounter, even more mysterious, another "outer stimulus for an upset," challenged how Ada would respond. Ada had just listened to a choir member as she reminisced and lamented about several unsuccessful auditions to sing in an opera. Because the singer had a beautiful voice, Ada recommended that she could still be enrolled in other famous chorus groups in the city. Less than ten minutes after parting to join others for a choral rendition, the singer came towards Ada's subgroup and blasted at her with such fury that others looked at Ada in shock and dismay as if she were the instigator! Ada did not respond, but was shocked and humiliated!

Orloff was right. The journey to self-knowledge can be humbling! Two rehearsals passed and the singer was absent. At the next session, she came to Ada and with a smile, apologized for her behavior. Her abusive behavior was public, yet her apology was quiet and private, unknown to the group. Ada accepted and gave her a hug, but the incident still left Ada flabbergasted and humiliated, wondering how on earth could such an amicable exchange ending with Ada's encouraging comments, give birth to such sudden, public verbal violence? Perhaps as a result of the apology, Ada became aware of a strange peace within her as she knew she had extended only good wishes and encouragement. Yet, she was left wondering again, why is she a target for such a raging outburst when she offered kindness? How did she draw such negativity? Another meaningful synchronicity. It seemed she was certainly being challenged emotionally and spiritually and more purification was necessary! Could this be related to the laundry room dream of purification she had several months before, where the room and fixtures were white, and all the workers were dressed in white doing the laundry?

> *I am standing in a huge laundry room. All the fixtures are in white; the people working there are all white and dressed in white clothing*. (Series C).

A third more prolonged interaction with a clergyman afforded one of Ada's most teachable and purifying experiences. She later realized more than ever, that the spotlight was then shining brightly on her at center stage, revealing the true status of her emotional self in an unfriendly relationship. While she admired the pastor, she felt resentment at some of his messages.

The two preceding encounters with a social worker and a singer must have been a prelude to a more poignant encounter that was imminent. Ada became very saddened that a sanctuary in a church she attended could become the station for repeated cynicism, demeaning, abusive language addressed indirectly, yet directly to specific members. A whole congregation was being held hostage to sermons interwoven with verbal weapons uttered from a sanctuary through one in a position of authority. It was not the first time that Ada wondered why a sanctuary should be used publicly for personal vendettas! Ada had said goodbye to another church for the same reason. There may have been other interesting sermons, but even one that is laced with bitterness and words with a "noxious explosion" reaching individuals seeking solace, can permanently alienate them from church and religion! There have been many such cases. Ada could still hear echoes of complaints from church members who had such experiences and had warned her. Why with such talent, use a sermon for toxic negativity when at the same moment, that sermon can be the perfect instrument for giving hope to people who have come from far distances, various backgrounds, enduring grief and tragedy, contributing to the collection basket, seeking hope, healing, spiritual nourishment, and rejuvenation?

At first Ada found herself becoming angry, but began studying her feelings and emotional reactions more closely. Was the pastor mirroring something within her? Why was she absorbing and becoming burdened with his negativity? Wasn't she making progress? Why does she feel that he is scrutinizing her? In her quest for self-understanding, Ada was reminded of Sechrist's comment, "we have a tendency to place all the blame on the faults of others because we can't admit to bad qualities within ourselves."[5]

No matter how he behaves, she must realize that his actions are his responsibility, and for those actions Ada must release her judgments, and focus on the good he is doing, and the divine within him. Yet, for reasons not entirely clear, Ada knew intuitively that some of those verbal missiles from the pulpit, were intended for her perhaps as reprimand for her seeming indifference. Despite the fact that both were active in a church environment, Ada realized that she and the pastor were emotionally trapped in a mutually sparked negative emotional vibration, which neither attempted to amicably reconcile. From her standpoint, her perceptions were shaping her judgments which sent her into emotional distancing mode! This reminded Ada of Cayce's dictum, "the thing that irritates you most in others is found in self! Else why would it bother you?"

Back to the negativity table, Ada became aware that dark emotions in her may have been attracting those in the pastor! In fact, without realizing it, Ada did not yet release the resentments she felt from the first two encounters! How can she overcome such vulnerability and be emotionally free? This is a conquest that is crucial to her advancement on her spiritual journey! This is no time to halt the digging!

Ada took further counsel from Gary Zukav's profound, mind-expanding book, *The Heart of the Soul,* regarding the human capacity for unconsciously wasting and misusing emotional energy based on negative judgments rooted in perceptions. As a result, strangely enough, Ada came to the point where she could admit and calmly observe her own feelings much more closely than she ever did before. At a later stage in examining herself, rather than feeling angry, threatened, or resentful, Ada's attitude became one of sadness and empathy both for herself and the pastor.

Thanks to further clarity given by Zukav who brilliantly points out that every emotion is a message or a signal from one's soul offering important information which no preacher, teacher, parent, or therapist can provide. For Ada, aspiring to experience emotional freedom, with continued delving like the otter to deepen her introspection, that information revealed those dynamics that she needed to identify, to acknowledge, and change from within herself, despite any upsetting external sources or circumstances. It is a matter of mental, physical, emotional, and spiritual health!

Regarding the relationship with the clergyman, Ada had two interesting dreams:

- *Walking with some people, I enter a church which is very cold. Long tubes of ice are on the floor; some are melting and there is water. I hear a sermon being preached but punctuated by recordings. Near the podium, dressed in vestments, a pastor with white hair, grey beard and thick eyebrows, sits shivering with a shawl over his shoulders. I hear someone say that it is cold but the heat is coming up.*

- *I am driving up a high hill and come to a sudden, wide curve. I am driving very fast and I am near the edge where I could swerve into the vast ocean far below. But I believe I am guided and I safely drive down the steep hill which follows the curve. Then below on the level after a gentle landing, I am surprised to be alive. I see another driver coming around the bend down the hill then crashes into a ditch!*

It is Cayce's view, endorsed by Kaplan, that dreams carry meanings on different levels. In the first dream, Ada wondered whether her distant attitude from the pastor was reflected by the coldness in the church and the pastor's shivering. A change in Ada's outlook seemed to be represented by the report that "the heat is coming up," indicating more warmth towards him. But was the sermon "punctuated by recordings," related to the pastor's deviation from the real, more inspirational sermon which comes from Spirit?

In the second dream, Ada at first believed that in her difficult climbing, that is, her efforts to gain self-knowledge and spiritually grounded emotional freedom, she was guided and protected from danger, "the vast ocean far below," by landing safely. The other driver whom she believed to be the pastor following her, "crashes into a ditch" as a result of his negative comments and the alienation felt by many other congregants.

However, on another level of meaning, driving fast uphill, skillfully avoiding the ocean below, and landing gently thus feeling glad to be alive, seemed to represent Ada's improving emotional self. The second driver which crashed could well represent the resentments and protective aloofness, self-sabotaging emotional issues which once "drove" her, were "ditched" or abandoned.

In effect, the experience of adversity with the clergyman had in it a precious jewel – the fact that Ada's former conditioning to place all clergymen on a pedestal, as authorities who were high and impeccable on the spiritual ladder, had settled into a new reality. Yet, she must retain the fact that they too were still instruments for good. Moreover, the pastor's attitude, the medium for reflecting her emotional imbalance, rather than feeling justified, became for Ada, the doorway to a level of transcendence "beyond intellectual knowing" where he is embraced from afar in the light and warmth of love, wishing for him "the good and the beautiful."

Thanks Mom, in my dream you did open a door to a lighted pathway and invited me to go through it. I now realize I was supposed to delve deep like the otter into the meanings of the lessons from the above encounters, beyond the doorway of light towards finding new understandings and levels of the "good and the beautiful" within.

If we walk away from the lessons, Breathnach warns, "they will only reappear in the next relationship until we recognize what's going on."[6] For Ada, it seemed all three encounters were meant as repeated lessons, blatant teaching experiences demanding attention for further rigorous self-study!

CHAPTER TWENTY-TWO

When you do not recognize your deeper painful emotions for what they are, they shape your perceptions, judgments, and actions. Zukav [1]

An unhealthy, unattended human emotional body is like a crack in our spiritual vessel. It creates an internal split that is deadly, both for us and those near to us. If we shatter while journeying on the spiritual path, it's usually because there was an undetected flaw in the emotional system that was not addressed in the early stages. Kaplan [2]

THE SYNCHRONICITIES: MORE REFLECTIONS AND LESSONS

Looking back on the timed, short succession of experiences with a social worker, a choir member, and a minister, Ada did not choose to fly into fits of anger, or impulsively retaliate with violence as a result of being bullied and battered by "emotional vampires," but she undoubtedly felt the impact of abuse and negativity and had a great urge to be purged of them. It was at a later stage in her self-study that she began experiencing a new feeling of peace, a gratitude for all her attackers, past and present. She had a renewed respect for the invisible, unknown benevolent forces which arranged the synchronicities, because each encounter, she later realized, enabled an inner transmutation, melting her own inwardly seething emotional reactions. What Sechrist asserts becomes highly relevant: "God permits only those experiences in our lives which are necessary for our greater growth and integration."[3]

Ada thought she had only kind feelings towards the social worker and the singer, but they showed Ada, that without constant vigilance and awareness of her emotional self, she can send a harmful energy to others despite her calm exterior. She distanced and "protected" herself and ignored her true, embedded emotions, an attitude which she repeated with the pastor from whom she had to learn again that her emotional distancing also carried a nested dark energy with a frequency that affected others. While that energy was not verbally expressed, it was expelled from her being to others with an equally damaging effect.

All three were teachers, who unconsciously participated in directing and spurring the synchrony of vibrations and movement Ada needed to be on the way towards experiencing, questioning, and understanding a higher level of emotional freedom, the catalyst and significant nutrient necessary for her spiritual advancement.

These encounters exemplify Orloff's description of "energy fields overlapping," of "synchronicities as a form of grace," and "moments of perfect timing," when "energetic forces" were aligned to assist Ada emotionally. Breathnach also provides another interesting view by stating, "...soul directed events defy logic and ridicule reason...authentic moments never betray us...they may leave us in a daze and catapult us into confusion...if you keep your heart steady...you can make it until the fog lifts...you can see the road again...see where you are headed...You are returning to Self."[4] Ada was convinced that the three encounters were "soul directed," did "defy logic," and they directed her to where the fog was lifting where she could "see the road again."

Ada's level of emotional awareness was further advanced as she viewed OWN on Sunday, Aug. 26th, 2012 when Oprah interviewed Rev. Ed Bacon, pastor of All Saints Episcopal Church, Texas. In discussing the difficulty of loving one's enemies and restraining from possible ego responses to attackers, such as "I'm gonna get him," or "Who do they think they are," etc., both agreed that such attitudes of revenge cause one to "fall asleep," to surrender one's power, thus contributing to the cycle of violence. Instead, one could choose to be awake, take a deep breath, step back, observe, and recognize that the moment of being attacked, could be "one of one's holiest moments" and recognize that "something sacred is at stake." In such a moment, choosing peace instead of retaliating with violence is emotional empowerment exercised in love and harmony, rather than with its opposite, anger rooted in fear. Undoubtedly, Ada concluded, this has to be a commitment of the spiritual traveler on the way to union with Self. This explanation gave Ada extended appreciation for and a renewed commitment to one of her parents' admonitions: Do not render evil for evil.

Ada became aware that although her responses to her attackers appeared non-violent and were not bearing attitudes of revenge, she was not yet awake, because she bore resentment, and initially did not recognize those moments as sacred opportunities for transcendence. In being emotionally distant, she was "asleep" and had surrendered her true power. She had yet to work towards "the death of the ego, death of all beliefs that separate you from others," as Ferrini explains, and recognize that "what dies is not you...what dies is everything you thought you were. Every judgment you ever made about yourself or anyone else. And what is born again is full of light and clarity...Christ that has eternal life in you and me"[5]. That statement nailed it on the head and also clarified for Ada what St. Paul meant when he said, "I die daily," which was re-stated regarding dying to the ego or false self in the peace prayer of St. Francis of Assisi, "It is in dying that we are born to eternal life."

With such incremental understanding, Ada's prophetic dream which she had years before was being fulfilled, attaining full significance, and with confident assurance:

While standing, I am looking at a badly shattered mirror!

Her previous and once 'secure' knowledge of herself was on the way to being radically shattered, altered, undergoing a sea-change. Caught in the flurry of everyday activities for survival, how distant Ada was even then, at the time of that dream, from any understanding, much more the complete fulfillment of the meaning of the dream!

CHAPTER TWENTY-THREE

Becoming liberated from the bondage of negativity lets you realize your tremendous value as a person - achieving Emotional Freedom gives you ongoing access to your own power center during jubilant times and in adversity. Orloff [1]

Spiritual growth exists in that moment when you are consciously willing to pay the price of freedom. You must be willing at all times, in all circumstances, to remain conscious in the face of pain and to work with your heart by relaxing and remaining open. Singer [2]

PERSONALITIES, EMOTIONAL FREEDOM, AND TRANSFORMATION

In pondering the circumstances and events along her spiritual path, Ada often felt admiration for some famous people by reflecting on their courage in adversity. For those who scoff at or question the remoteness of emotional pain and suffering as a vehicle for transformation, they need only recall the global impact of some modern human life-changing events and personalities.

They can recall a few exemplars and mirrors of transcendent response to suffering and emotional freedom. Renowned psychiatrist, Viktor Frankl in *Man's Search For Meaning* describes how important it was to teach tortured and despairing, imprisoned men in a concentration camp a different attitude toward life, that "it did not really matter what we expected from life, but rather what life expected from us...our answer must consist...in right action and in right conduct."[3] Even more profoundly, he asserts that a man who becomes conscious of the responsibility he bears toward another human being who affectionately waits for him, or an unfinished work, he will never be able to throw away his life. He knows the 'why' for his existence, and will be able to bear almost any 'how.' According to Frankl, "life in a concentration camp tore open the human soul and exposed its depths,"[4] and at their most fragile stage of existence, fellow prisoners began to value each other as persons connected to one another in a space of seeming hopelessness.

Gandhi spent several hours of fasting and adapted a non-violent approach to successfully free India from the choking oppression of British colonialism without war. He was so emotionally free, that by his fasting, vision, and activism, he was willing to pay the price of freedom for India. Inspired by Gandhi, Martin Luther King, Jr. used a similar system to revolutionize Civil Rights in the United States of America. Despite frequent acts of brutality, imprisonment of innocent people and himself, in his last speech preceding his death, feeling emotionally free, King could declare "a holy moment" by his words, "I have seen the Promised Land!"

Doubters can also contemplate twenty seven years of inhumane prison experiences as prelude to Mandela's elevation to Prime Minister of South Africa. Willing to "work with the heart," armed only with spiritual tools of compassion, non-retaliation, and non-violence, and liberated from the negativity he once felt, Mandela became a one-man army which dismantled the oppressive regime of apartheid thus opening pathways to truth and reconciliation sessions. A democratic society was born.

Just as heroic was Pope John Paul, remembered for his love for all people. In a "holy moment" while visiting the prison, he extended sincere forgiveness to, and created a friendship with the one who deliberately but unsuccessfully attempted to assassinate him.

Ada later recognized that all these men, among others as mirrors, have taught the modern world the meaning of emotional freedom - how to be anchored in what Orloff refers to as "one's power center whether in adversity or in happiness." It is only from this center that one can honor the divinity in even the most cruel adversary. By his life, Mandela illustrated his belief that being free goes beyond casting off one's chains; it is also to live one's life in such a way that the freedom of others is also respected and promoted. For this reason, it is important to know just when it is necessary to tap one's power center, and how to locate it!

Apparently, this is not self-esteem based on class, status, body image, glamorous fashion, money, stardom, achievement, wealthy possessions, or romantic affairs.

Indeed, even after all these have been realized, one's power center is something much, much deeper. It is what Breathnach refers to as that Something More of authentic self-worth, authentic self-knowledge. It is "that mysterious, missing, odd-fitting piece of ourselves, and Spirit is determined we're going to find it one way or another."[5].

When one is anchored in one's power center, one is firmly rooted in invincible self-worth born of authentic self-knowledge, and as observed by Orloff, choices that we make are linked with our self-worth. Cayce's mandate to "study self, study self," became even more compelling for Ada.

Frankl, Gandhi, Martin Luther King, Pope John Paul II, Mandela, and others made choices that were compatible with their true self-worth, how they valued themselves and others, choices which stemmed from the power center within them that transcended the worst adversities that they lived through. Emotional pain and suffering then, can *indeed* become a doorway, a crucible through which a new dimension of self can be reached. When viewed consciously, it can become a purifying, fine tuning, elevating experience. Shakespeare had endorsed this centuries ago in *As You Like It,* where he stated "Sweet are the uses of adversity, which like the toad, ugly and venomous, Wears yet a precious jewel in his head." (Act II, Sc.1). When we "fall asleep" as Rev. Bacon stated, by acts of revenge, hate, violence, or in Ada's case, protective aloofness, we cannot see the precious jewel.

How can such an empowering shift to one's power center occur in a moment of threatening adversity and toxicity? The Buddhist concept of mindfulness, that honest, deep introspection, is one key to the change; bitterness, anger, resentment, jealousy, arrogance, revenge, inferiority/superiority complexes, all of which are offsprings of fear, are not only inhibiting, disempowering emotions, they destroy the possibility of awakening to the richest dimension of self on the journey.

In her landmark book, *Emotional Alchemy: How the Mind Can Heal the Heart*, Tara Bennett-Goleman provides further insight embedded in certain Buddhist practices. She explains that when we are confronted with the countless challenges and predicaments of life, the energies of our emotions are activated. It is by being mindful of those activated energies then, that they can be transmuted by channeling the emotions towards positive ends, thus producing an alchemical change similar to changing lead into gold. As a spiritual vehicle, the emotional energies can become engaged in the process of "spiritual alchemy."

By using such a method as spiritual alchemy, it is possible to eventually become like the Buddha who sat meditatively still under the bodhi tree while a huge elephant which was scaring people from their villages, came charging furiously towards him. The Buddha remained unmoved. To the amazement of the frightened, young attendant who warned him of the approaching danger, the snorting, enormous elephant abruptly arrived and knelt submissively in silence before the Buddha. The animal which charged so threateningly amid the screaming sounds of fear from villagers, became tranquilized and subdued in the presence of love and reverence from the Buddha, who after some moments, lovingly patted the huge animal on its forehead. This is one's power center in action!

This story reinforced for Ada an insight and a stage she zealously hopes to achieve in this lifetime: that when emotional freedom is truly attained, one is aware of no form of fear, only its transforming opposite, love. Secondly, she became more cognizant of the importance of mindfulness of her emotional energy. She was quite aware that her challenges could not even be remotely compared to the harsh realities endured by Frankl, Gandhi, King, the Pope, or Mandela. However, Frankl succinctly settles any such empty attempt at comparisons by stating, "...life's tasks are also very real and concrete. No man and no destiny can be compared with any other man or any other destiny. No situation repeats itself, and each situation calls for a different response"[6] Reinforcing the futility of comparison are the following messages from two of Ada's teachers:

> *...don't try to play someone else's role; play your own...knowing yourself is the source of change for your life. We change our reality by changing what is within us. This is our place of wholeness. The more we take responsibility for our reality, the quicker we will grow. Praagh*[7]
>
> *"The most common despair is...not choosing, or willing, to be oneself,"...Soren Kierkegaard warns us... "but the deepest form of despair is to choose to be another than oneself." This is how we always hurt the one we love. The one we shouldn't hurt at all. Our Self." Breathnach*[8]

A deeper personal understanding Ada realized was that the adversity she experienced in the various encounters were meant as teaching, mirroring, and purging agents along her journey, functioning to open the blocked pathways which were impediments to new levels of her self-knowledge.

A fine-tuning insight came from Kaplan's observation that "as our lives are falling apart...while all that seemingly devastating and deranging stuff is happening in our waking lives, that's when the healing dreams come. We sense a transfiguration that is leaving no stone unturned, no cell ignored. Our molecular structure is being changed, man."[9]. Thus, as Kaplan also captures so well, the purposeful encounters of various personalities occurred for Ada during *the destruction period to lay the foundation for the reconstruction"* directing her new sense of self. As in her precognitive dream of "the shattered mirror" years before, Ada's previous self was truly being altered in preparation for an awakening!

Perhaps this also explains the paradoxes between Ada's thorny interactions with others ("devastating and deranging") and her many positive dreams of a male or female guardian clothed in white, of flowers, birds, rain, scooping honey, music in so many forms, in addition to singing children, etc., seemingly without logic. In truth, the positive dreams were healing dreams, heralding and working for the reconstruction of her inner self.

It was in the course of digging into the *What* and the *When* of her dreams that Ada could appreciate the wide range of personalities, synchronistic encounters, richly woven into the fabric of her life particularly at times of confusion and disharmony, forcing her to examine her emotional landscape, taking inventory of the "inner" to identify how it corresponded with the "outer." In so doing, she could also appreciate Dr. Orloff's reference to "overlapping energy fields, synchronicities as a form of grace, and the perfect timing of inspired coincidences, and the startling precision with which things fall into place."[10].

Ada believed that among others, the examples of her encounter with a social worker, a singer, and a clergyman, validate emotional inquiry as "spiritual strengthening," but even more importantly, how **"the emotions you are working with will shape the synchronicities you experience ...such auspicious intersections are bonafide intuitive moments when energetic forces align via synchronicities to assist you emotionally."[11] . This is profound and truly awesome despite the fact that in the harshness of some of those synchronicities, Ada wished to bellow and scream at her loudest! However, she believed that in her dig for the *Why*, she had uncovered a significant find – the state of her emotions reflects her level of spiritual attunement.

Ada was aware of such activity like an undercurrent, silent, mysterious, whispering stream secretly flowing within her, oddly felt, and known only to herself. Her waking life, aptly explained by Kaplan**, was "undergoing radical redirection,"**... " a complete transformation, and you start to live a life that is in alignment with your soul's intent."[12]. This realization of redirection was not in her consciousness then, but in retrospect, was unmistakably occurring for Ada.

Self-Knowledge and Lessons

As Frankl points out, no two persons travel identical paths because the means and circumstances for learning the lessons need to be different. Similar to Christian in John Bunyan's *Pilgrim's Progress,* obstacles, suffering, and challenges contain lessons and opportunities to help to transform the limited self-knowledge of the spiritual traveler. Like Christian, it is important to remain undeterred on the way to finding the Celestial City, the real one within, which is everyone's journey, including Ada's.

What happens when we ignore the lessons? As previously mentioned, Gary Zukav emphasizes that missing the lessons in the Earth School or ignoring them retards our progress, and the lessons will reappear and repeat until the light bulb moment arrives. Wilda Tanner puts it another way when she refers to the interactive nature of relationships and the ongoing process of these relationships which act as our mirrors, and "when we fail to get the message, or worse, refuse to heed it, the dynamics become more aggressive and the reflections are more exaggerated..."[13]. Consequently, in the course of her inner explorations, Ada became quite aware that she had a serious responsibility for advancing her progress and fulfilling her spiritual purpose in the Earth School which Zukav explains as the challenge to strive for the "personality to be in alignment with the soul." What must not be forgotten is that the personality is the vehicle for expressing one's full range of emotions.

Once again Ada thought, "Thanks Mom! In my dream you opened a door to a lighted pathway and invited me to go through it. I now realize I was supposed to be engaged in and be transformed by all the adventures leading to 'the good and the beautiful!,' which includes emotional freedom!"

CHAPTER TWENTY-FOUR

You may not grasp the importance of a teaching dream for many years, indeed, you may not even understand the message for a long time. Kaplan.[1]

Emotional awareness and spiritual growth develop together. As you become aware of everything you are feeling all of the time, you embark upon the path of spiritual growth. You cannot embark upon this path and remain ignorant of your emotions. Zukav.[2]

SOME PREDICTIVE DREAMS AND MESSAGES

Already mentioned is Cayce's reference to the "self-regulating, self-enhancing, self-training" nature of dreams, and that they come to provide "an experience" for the dreamer, and to effect change. In retrospect, even when she did not understand them, Ada's dreams were subconsciously providing her with unique experiences leading to inner change.

In the early part of this book, Ada described two predictive dreams, one related to spaceships which preceded a family reunion, and another of two exotic birds related to her trips to two different countries. She understood the meanings and messages long after the fact. This predictive quality continued. In considering the "the body of dreams" and patterns, the following examples selected from their respective series were not immediately understood, but are now viewed with greater clarity. Echoing through the years, in her pursuit of self-knowledge, they seem to relate to her yearning to understand and experience emotional freedom in connection with her evolving spirituality.

> **Series A: *There is a healthy plant growing out of a wall and as I look at it, it extends a branch with flower buds already opening to bloom.***

> **Series B: *While standing, I am looking at a badly shattered mirror.***

> **Series C: *I am driving with two others and pass over some huge rocks rather smoothly. Then I take a perpendicular path as though***

it were a vertical wall. I feel a great deal of support from the right – unbelievable, all the way up until I reach the top where the view is a beautiful plain. What a relief when I get there!

Series D: I am ascending some steps. Figures dressed in white are passing me up and down and I am being helped to the top. On one side there is a mountain and a beautiful valley with a beautiful scene dominated by a church.

Series G: I am being pulled up, up, up through clouds; I look at the scene below and I think, "How beautiful!" I feel suspended and others are floating with me.

Series J: I hear the most beautiful harmony of voices from the upstairs of a house – I wish to join them. A tall buxom woman comes down the stairs in my direction and says, "You've just begun to live your life!"

In contrast to her former low level of self-knowledge when Ada first arrived in New York in 1976, most of these dreams through the years predicted an upward movement of her life, ascending, climbing, seemingly towards slowly realizing a more spiritually mature understanding of herself.

She now believes she was depicted as the "healthy plant" with buds getting ready to bloom. "The badly shattered mirror" indicated the destruction of her false sense of self. A new view of herself which Ada could not have envisioned would be found far beyond the former boundaries when, in her dream, she was told by the woman on the stairs, "You've just begun to live your life."

While she was uncertain of most of her dreams, it became evident that they were telling a story of a future level of soul-growth through the many recurring climbing symbols, especially climbing a vertical wall with support, ascending steps, speedily riding a bike over a hill, or pulled up, up among clouds

Before settling in New York, her attempts in a dream to climb a rock left her bruised and bleeding, warning of the need for change which she had ignored. Subsequent climbing in dreams seemed at first to indicate her academic and professional advancement. However, even after those levels were achieved, the climbing symbols frequently continued far beyond in the reach to greater self-knowledge where her spirituality and greater intimacy with her emotions were evolving into sacred companionship with Spirit. Being told in a dream, "Ada, you have just begun to live your life," reflected imminent change within herself, a distant threshold yet to be attained. Without the slightest clue of what she would encounter, in her retirement years she stood ready with eagerness and openness for more spiritually enlightening adventures.

CHAPTER TWENTY-FIVE

When we pay attention to the emotional content of our dreams we have the opportunity to resolve our deeper feelings and recover more quickly from life's emotional crises. Barrick [1]

Emotional freedom is an inner peace movement that is birthed within us then emanates into the world. The starting place is you. The more peace you enjoy, the more that peace ripples to everyone. Orloff [2]

CHANGES, NEW KNOWLEDGE, AND DREAMS

For about three years, Ada had been searching and making preparations for a new place to live definitely knowing that she would soon leave New York where she had lived and worked for thirty years. There was no doubt in her mind that the purpose and cycle for residing in that city had been completed. By personal choice, she initially settled briefly in north Florida, then under the most mysterious circumstances designed by Providence, she was led to Central Florida in a receptive caring community where spiritual groups flourish. New friends engaged in spiritual advancement entered her life, giving a freshness and emotional aliveness she had not felt for a long time and could not anticipate. Often recalling the story of the Buddha, Ada continued to pursue her journey to experiencing emotional freedom which, she became convinced, is linked with one's level of spirituality. She attended group discussions on *A Course in Miracles,* enrolled in a Spiritual Psychology Retreat, completed a course on Transcendental Meditation, attended lectures at the Tree of Life, and enrolled in a 15-month program of Mystery School Teachings.

The combination of mind-expanding, elevating teachings from these sources flew open other doors of illumination on the fundamental link between emotional freedom, the spiritual, and the authentic self, which Zukav describes as "the alignment of the personality with the soul." However, as rich as these experiences had been, more was yet to come, a new windfall, and it seemed dreams had always been pointing the way!

More Dreams Pointing the Way – SERIES Q

About six months before her arrival in Florida in 2007, Ada had several interesting predictive dreams. With nebulous understanding at best and without any immediate event to which they may be associated, she was unable then to decipher their exact meanings, but she continued to record them. She could only wait, while guessing that something favorable was afoot, uncertain what shape or form it would take or when. In her dreams, as Cayce had stated, themes and patterns would repeat with variations in "the body of dreams." The following are a few of those dreams:

Audience:

- *I am facing a large, expectant crowd, waiting for an event. They are to participate in a song someone must first teach them. I am walking across the stage as if the responsibility is on my shoulders. I hear myself saying, as if ready and confident to teach the crowd, "O.K., just give me a microphone."*

One of the activities Ada engaged in after settling in Florida was giving workshops based on the spiritual psychology teachings she received in Missouri by Dr. Michael Ryce, "Why does This Happen To Me Again." Those sessions proved informative and enriching for attendees and rewarding for Ada.

At first, Ada believed that the following four dreams were echoes of the work she had done with children.

Children and Music:

- *A child sits at a piano and plays a melody. It is a huge interior space and I am going up some short steps listening to the melody and hearing the echo of several singing voices.*

- *I am standing with some people. From a distance, two children, about 9 to 11 years, break through the group, run towards me and hug me very closely. I don't think I met them before but I am overcome with their presence and love.*

- *A young boy child with curly hair comes into my view. I hear him sing a single high note. It is a rich and beautiful sound.*

- *Many children are in a large auditorium, and someone near the front is playing the piano. The music is fast, wonderful, but unfamiliar. As if on cue the children rise, walk in orderly formation while they are singing and the sound is heavenly.*

A closer examination of the connection of children with singing, harmony, and expressions of love led Ada to the awareness or reflection of qualities in children which she deeply seeks to enjoy, and yearns to cultivate and live with in her being. Her choice of a new location turned out to be one which would afford her opportunities to foster such qualities.

Dreams related to Lights and Movement provide another interesting study. These dreams predicted the various spiritual courses that Ada would be involved in, e.g. Transcendental Meditation and more than a year's course in Mystery School Teachings of the East. This was represented by the angels as messengers "dancing and playing violins," bringing illumination as the "brightly lit sky, with silvery light." The theme is continued in the "crystal city" or "city of lights."

The presence of Asians underscored the eastern teachings as well as the spiritual element of a "holy man" in long white garments. Ada's position of elevation on the summit of a hill indicated her new level of consciousness as a result of the teachings she would receive in her new location.

Lights:

- *I am looking at a brightly lit sky with silvery light, narrow, horizontal streaks of clouds. In front against this backdrop are three angels in silvery white garments trimmed with gold at the sides. They are dancing and playing violins.*

- *I am in an elevated area. I walk to the summit of the hill where a city is being built and I think of "crystal city" or "city of lights." There are Asians, and one is uncoiling a material with tassels. A tall, white male in long, white garment appears. We see each other as he walks toward the lights. As our eyes meet I think he must be a holy man.*

Movement:

- *I am climbing a ladder and I am amazed at how fast I am going. I come to a part with more difficulty near the top, but I make it. Someone is behind me doing the climb but more slowly.*

- *On a small vehicle more like a bike, I am going up a steep hill and I need to reach the top. My first attempt is not good, so I return to the bottom of the hill, pick up speed and ride straight to the top without problem.*

- *I haven't driven for many years yet I am driving a large car filled with children over rough terrain. One woman in a library says she overheard a male commenting on the driving as being advanced in skill.*

In the dreams of Movement, Ada's climbing and biking with speed, and her elevation to the top of a hill reinforced the pending exposure to new and transformative teachings. By driving skilfully, she was in confident control of the direction she had chosen and the sense of progressive fulfillment of the 'something more' for which she had been yearning.

It is not surprising that Nature as a theme was again represented in Ada's dreams before leaving New York. She found the first dream below very striking as it is the second time that she had a dream with almost exact content. Ada considers herself an amateur swimmer therefore she stays away from deep water. In this dream, without fear, she followed her guide through the deep to the ocean floor to meet an angelic being. Ada now believes that again, there is a message of expanded consciousness to be expected, and she would continue to be directed to those experiences. Later in this narrative, a full explanation will be given of the rich and varied teachings from Teachers expressed as fairies and angels or messengers in the second dream.

Nature:

- *There is a large body of clear, light blue water. Light is shining through it, and I am aware of a being in white who guides me downwards straight through the water. We are abreast of each other with arms straight ahead diving to the ocean floor. The being vanishes; it is like daylight down there, and I feel the gentle undulating movement of the water. I am on my knees as I face a beautiful, young, child-like angelic being with a pleasant, peaceful, loving, half-smiling face. Our eyes meet, and I think we are communicating telepathically, but I really don't know what is being said.* (Ada had this dream once before).

- *I am looking at a white winter fairyland all covered with snow of whitest white. A winding path is made through it, and on either side are figures like dancing fairies and angels with gilded edged wings. I reach out as if to gather the angels who then seem to become toys.*
- *I am looking at a garden with tall crape myrtle trees. They have huge, projecting, lush orange blossoms, stretching forward as if forcing to get my attention.*
- *A long, high area is in full bloom with cherry pink crape myrtle blossoms!*

It was with much surprise when Ada discovered that the last two dreams were in reality describing the stretches of multi-colored crape myrtle flowering plants which would be found in abundance during summer in the neighborhood where she would finally settle. Besides the dominance of green representing potential growth and aliveness, the colors of purple, orange, and pink symbolized the possibilities for the balance of emotional and spiritual feelings.

Quite often in Ada's dreams are tall, benevolent men as in the first two dreams in the group of *Strange Figures*. "Holding my hand" seemed to indicate she was being led and guided. In the second, the house represented Ada. Her spirit guide as protector and comforter, was unconcerned although the house was burning, indicating the destruction of her emotional hang-ups, inhibitions, and negative experiences which had not served her purposes for spiritual progress. She was being guided towards a promising new phase of her life .

Strange Figures:

- *I am walking beside a very tall man about 10' tall. He is holding my hand and looking down at me. We smile; his eyes are blue and his lanky figure reminds me of Peter O'Toole in the movie, Lawrence of Arabia.*

- *I am walking toward another place with a gentleman beside me. I look behind and the house we were both in is on fire. The house is old and the flame is quickly spreading. The gentleman beside me shows absolutely no concern.*

- *Someone is fitting me with a full-length long-sleeved dress. It is as though I am being prepared for something.*

- *A tall, white woman stands in front of me, dressed in white with trimmings of gold around her neck and hip. I say to her, "You are gorgeous! You look like a goddess!" Another lady, also beautifully dressed, seems to have hosted a gathering. I receive a beautiful gift – a deep blue heart-shaped glass, which I put into a secret place.*

As the events evolved later, indeed, Ada was "being prepared for something." The woman dressed in white "with trimmings of gold around her neck," an item of value sparked Ada's animated utterances, and another gave her a gift as if to emphasize what is to come.

When she examined the patterns in this "body of dreams" from a total perspective, she had no doubt that most of them conveyed positive messages. Even when she was in danger of men throwing black balls at her, she was unharmed and able to elude them as a seeming act of emotional triumph. This dream seemed to indicate victory over her inhibitions,

> *I am on a country road with trees on both sides. Some men are following me and I doubt their intentions. A dominant one wants my support in a political activity and I refuse. As I walk up a hill, he and his allies begin to throw black balls at me. They land near and around me but none explodes as I fear. I elude his men who went ahead as if to ambush me.*

This dream was in marked contrast to a previous attack dream where Ada encountered physical assault and was entangled in withes and knots after she announced her retirement.

It was clear that the declarative message given by a woman in Ada's dream several months before, "you have just begun to live your life!" meant a new phase of her life was about to begin! Did that mean more climbing? Perhaps Ada needed to review and examine more closely the insights of the previous phases of her adventure leading to the current level in order to be aware and be prepared for what may yet be ahead in the dig.

CHAPTER TWENTY-SIX

To search within, to truly understand oneself, to foster a sense of detachment and perspective-these are difficult tasks and they require patience and much practice. The journey is arduous and long, but well worth it. Weiss [1]

CLUES, FINDINGS, SHIFTS IN SELF-KNOWLEDGE SO FAR ON THE JOURNEY

PHASE ONE – A Yearning for Something More and a Changing Identity

1. Spiritual communication occurs not just through dreams but also concretely through flowers, e.g. a begonia which first evoked Ada's desire to bloom.

2. Dreams are personal communication lines conveying messages expressing, predicting, directing one's pathway to higher reaches of inner being and becoming. Eastern teachings opened new ways of thinking.

PHASE TWO – Intellectual Achievement Vs. Spiritual Growth

3. When intellectual goals are pursued with good intentions, guidance is provided from the spirit world. Symbolized in a dream, Ada was led to a professor who became the door leading to the publishing of an academic text. Satisfying experiences resulted from the endeavor.

4. A consuming preoccupation with achievement, certain intellectual pursuits, and ego attachments can alienate an individual from the in-depth self-knowledge necessary for advancing one's spiritual growth.

5. Depending on the individual personality, religious beliefs, frequent attendance at church, listening to sermons, rites and ceremonies may have only a superficial impact on the seeker's growth, and true self-understanding can be thwarted. Other sources of truth are needed to expand one's thinking. Religion, though helpful, can be constricting; spirituality is

soul-elevating. Listening to the spiritual persuasions of Eastern teachers opened a new doorway for Ada. Her dreams of Asians, old and new slippers were enlightening symbols.

6. All relationships, especially those which seemingly evoke conflicts, serve as prisms and reflect brilliant opportunities for self-knowledge. They are catalysts for promoting an inner metamorphosis. Each becomes a teaching experience for self-study, emotional awareness through deep intimacy and honesty with one's feelings. Ada realized this after several lessons from various encounters.

PHASE THREE –Shift to a new level of Consciousness

7. Attention to feelings and emotions in dreams is imperative as they reflect "the needs of the personality in service to one's soul" on the long journey to alignment, balance, and authenticity.

8. The peace, love, and harmony one hungers for are not dependent on outer events, people, or status, seeking to impress others, or gain approval although they are part of life. Happiness does not occur when one is imprisoned by false standards of superiority and inferiority. Rather, wholeness occurs from within by cleansing one's energy system of disempowering negative emotions which can lead to spiritual impoverishment.

9. In dreams, how we respond to charged emotional moments reveal whether we are spiritually retrogressing or advancing.

PHASE FOUR – More Insights into Self-Discovery

10. Valuing self and expressing reverence for all life in thought, word and action, contribute to positive energy frequencies which benefit everyone.

11. Once seriously committed to the journey towards wholeness, adversities will come from unexpected sources, some without any apparent reason, but serving to teach, test, and strengthen the dreamer. The dreamer should not be frightened, but armed and ready to consciously engage each encounter, each moment, as a sacred opportunity, a holy gift in the dance towards spiritual advancement. The dreamer now understands that all experiences, including adverse ones are in service with perfection for the benefit of the soul.

12. At an enriched level of self-understanding comes humility, a calm attitude, a release, a unique engagement with inner peace and a feeling of being surrounded by omnipresent love. "Be still and know that I am God" (Ps. 46: 10) beckons with acute awareness and conviction.

Although Ada was aware of the above phases in her explorations, the yearning for "something more" continued to be strongly felt. Apparently, the dig must go on to the next phase.

CHAPTER TWENTY-SEVEN

In personal dreaming we are asked to broaden personal belief systems and to mature spiritually...ask us to grow, to open our minds, to open those letters!...expand one's belief system so deeper truths can be accessed. Kaplan[1]

If a man desires to receive God's approval, it is his duty to try not only to understand himself, but also understand his individual relationship to others. This he can do through the reception of messages from higher forces, as in dreams...for the best development of the human family, greater increase in knowledge of the subconscious soul or spirit world is necessary. Sechrist[2]

INSIGHTS LEADING TO THE WHY

Ada was fortunate to be introduced in her childhood to the spirit world by her Mom who first revealed to her the wisdom of dreams. Actually, Ada was given a gift just by example and a Mom's sharing. Her capacity for interpreting her dreams was born of sheer, deep intuitive connection with her soul reflected in her character as a simple, humble, spiritually attuned individual. Ada is aware that her relationship with her mother has impacted her life of dreams, thus influencing her desire for increased knowledge for spiritual development.

The hundreds of dreams which flooded Ada's life were meant to guide her along a heroine's inner archaeological journey into her own singular, spiritual universe. She traversed shifting routes from first relying on external factors for a sense of self, resulting in a limited view of self-understanding based on cultural patterns and conditioning to professional achievements, then further to pathways with greater focus on knowledge of her emotional self in interaction with others. She at last recognized that the enigma of emotional freedom was a key factor intertwined with knowing herself spiritually, yet still challenging her search was the *why* of her dreams!

Mom's frequent visits to Ada from the other side "bringing messages from higher forces" were assurances of continued support, healing, and encouragement on the difficult journey towards realizing what is really important as the *Why* of her dream journey.

A Bouquet Gives A Lesson

Despite the many vicissitudes in her life from which Ada can draw many lessons, she now realizes that her blooming towards emotional freedom could not be instantaneous, not a sudden transformation into a new version of herself. Ada could not help but recall the sacred moments she once spent in the presence of a bouquet of Merostar lilies, a precious birthday gift from friend, Bonnie. From the table on which the vase with the bouquet lay, a faint sound drew Ada's attention, just in time for her to watch the miracle of one lily after another unfolding its petals, as if reflecting the process of what her imminent blooming would be like - a delicate, gradual unfolding from each new experience like the petals of the lily! Each stage, each unfolding was gently ushered by new encounters or circumstances, sometimes painful, sometimes joyful; each was playing a part, and all were being subconsciously observed, nurtured, treasured, reflected on, and savored. Each experience was giving empowerment, providing new insight and energy in preparation for the next. Ada's blooming would be unique, highly personal, intriguing, while relentlessly crossing her silently mindful radar of emotional awareness.

Three Guiding Principles

Through personal comments and her remarkable book, *The Invisible Garment*, Dr. Connie Kaplan describes thirteen principles that are woven into the fabric of human life. These principles are "downloaded information" as a rare gift from her deceased grandfather. The author identified three of those principles which permeate Ada's dreams as primary patterns: regeneration, peace, and flowering. After much reflection, Ada was convinced that these principles had been directing her long inner journey spanning many years.

Kaplan explains that regeneration occurs when we recreate ourselves physically and psychologically. Ada was often spiritually recharged when she organized innovative professional conferences and activities, but especially when she visited various energy sites and expanded her knowledge of spiritual truths beyond the boundaries of organized religion. A special moment of psychological regeneration occurred when Ada stood facing one of the world's most imposing structures, the Taj Mahal in Agra, India. The mausoleum, referred to as "a monument to love," was built by grief-stricken Emperor Shah Jahan to honor his wife Muntaz, who died during childbirth. Ada gazed with utter amazement at the spectacular representation of symmetric artistic and architectural perfection, and in that moment believed that it is a symbolic microcosm of the universe in which all of creation, is a monument to love, a perfect manifestation of the Creator.

In her activities with children, Ada was guided by the principle of peace. The many repetitive nature symbols in her dreams of flowers, waterfalls, birds, streams, and light reflect this principle. Of all three, flowering, the principle of gradual evolution, speaks loudest. Flowering connects with both regeneration and peace in the gradual unfolding of Ada's life in her search for 'something more' or what was missing. In subtle ways, the three principles had been operating to nourish the blooming and subconsciously directing her inner adventure. The following dreams can now be reexamined as highly reflective of the principles, together with their meanings, which had eluded her when they occurred!

> *There is a healthy plant growing out of a wall and as I look at it,*
> *it extends a branch with flower buds already opening to bloom.*
> *I call a man nearby to come and see the unusual spectacle!*
> (Series A, 4)

I hear the most beautiful harmony of voices from the upstairs of a house. I wish to join them. A tall buxom woman comes down the stairs in my direction and says, "You've just begun to live your life!" (Series J, 7).

There is a large body of clear, light blue water. Light is shining through it and I am aware of a being in white who guides me downwards straight through the water. We are abreast of each other with arms straight ahead diving to the ocean floor. The being vanishes; it is like daylight down there and I feel the gentle undulating movement of the water. I am on my knees as I face a beautiful, young child-like, angelic being with a pleasant, peaceful, loving, half-smiling face. Our eyes meet, and I think we are communicating telepathically, but I really don't know what is being said. (Series Q, Nature,1). *This dream occurred twice.*

Without realizing it, a healthy plant growing out of an arid wall and extending itself with buds, music, and a dictum, "You've just begun to live your life!" were revealing Ada's regeneration and flowering principles at work. In the third, which some teachers refer to as a numinous dream, the peace principle could not be more evident than diving through clear water, escorted into light and in the presence of angelic beauty and innocence! All three dreams seemed to engender a promise of emergence toward a new level of spiritual self. But Ada did not give them the attention they deserved! However, the messages intended by these dreams and principles would be extended later into more concrete events.

CHAPTER TWENTY-EIGHT

Joy is permanent. Happiness is temporary. Joy depends on what happens inside of you. Happiness depends on what happens outside of you...Happiness requires changing circumstances, including people. Joy requires changing yourself. Zukav.[1]

Only you can reach your goal [spiritual fulfillment], because ultimately our journey home is an inward journey, a personal return...Because the kingdom of heaven exists within us, all joy and happiness come from within ourselves...As we experience true love and become enlightened, we will "save" ourselves. Weiss.[2]

NOURISHMENT FOR
THE BLOOMING

Having abandoned some of the old restricting beliefs of religion and tasted the richness of teachings from several other spiritual philosophies, Ada was poised to embrace that ever elusive "something more." She was led further to other messengers whose teachings beckoned her to accommodate deeper knowledge, and whose wisdom revealed truths which helped to satisfy her need to experience emotional freedom, providing her with a puzzling, yet unusual lightness of spirit.

Two Significant Messages

Among the latest teachings which had a great impact on Ada, two had an all-encompassing effect. The first, Gregg Braden, internationally famous author and speaker, is among the few messengers bridging science and spirituality at this time of cosmic change. Ada learned from him some illuminating ideas which had a great impact on her self-understanding and changed how she perceived herself emotionally.

He referred to the teaching of the Ancients, the Essenes, who taught their listeners to trust the process of life and regard the Dark Night of the Soul as an opportunity "to lose everything we have ever held dear...to see ourselves in the presence and nakedness of that nothing, and as we climb ourselves out of the abyss of that nothing from everything we have lost, we see ourselves in a new way; that is where we find ourselves at the highest levels of mastery."[3] When Ada felt frustrated with herself despite all she had achieved years earlier, if she had heard this teaching, her plight would have been worse out of sheer ignorance of the deep truth embedded in that statement. Now, Ada recognizes the extent to which her previous ego attachments were obstacles to her blooming.

Braden shared another more profound and healing teaching of the Essenes called The Blessing, defined as a "quality of thought, feeling, and emotion." The Blessing is predicated on the fact that "when we bless an event that has hurt us, or an individual that has caused us pain or grief," we are acknowledging "the divine or sacred nature of all that has unfolded, and that it is divine and sacred by virtue of being part of the One, the single Source of all that is." Again, the idea of a holy moment, an instant of grace to be alive is affirmed.

However, Braden continued more explicitly to give unique clarity about how this tool works. He states that the Gift of the Blessing is our opportunity to "free the charge that the hurt caused in our bodies so that we can move forward towards life's other offerings." This does not mean agreeing to, or condoning what occurred, and we "may not understand where it fits, and how it fits, and in that there is release." The Blessing occurs by looking directly into the face of the pain "that brought you to the depths of darkness" and say, "I bless this." Braden refers to this as "emotional empowerment," and it takes a powerful person to do such an act. In other words, as Tammy Goben, a medium explains, the charge of the negative emotion causes a blockage which prevents the healing currents of love to flow into one's system. Letting go of the charge is important for healing.

For all who seek to experience their best selves while living in a world where conflict is a daily reality in the workplace, in families, boardrooms and institutions, Braden's message of emotional empowerment is timely. Recalling the many times when Ada held resentment, such a concept as The Blessing resounded as an ideal strategy for attaining emotional freedom.

The Blessing corroborates the explanation of Dr. Orloff, a second teacher who maintains that "emotional freedom is the fertilizer that makes blooming possible." After referring to Gwendolyn Brooks' statement to "Conduct your blooming in the noise and whip of the whirlwind," Dr. Orloff declares, "That's what emotional freedom is all about: your blooming."[4] In other words, there is a direct link between one's potential to bloom, suffering, and emotional freedom! To bloom then is to be emotionally free! When one can transcend and sublimate the most adverse circumstances, that is blooming! That is what Oprah and Ed Bacon had agreed to as a holy moment when the blockage caused by negativity in emotional pain is released by blessing it! Emotional freedom is what the Buddha symbolized under the Bodhi tree when the enormous elephant came charging towards him! That is what Frankl, Gandhi, King, Pope John, and Mandela found – a kind of "stargate" to a new realm of self on the way to meet Self. In the "noise and whip of the whirlwind" of their circumstances, they epitomized emotional freedom.

Ada is now at a point in her inner journey where she can wholeheartedly embrace these teachings with a resounding "Yes! I rejoice and I am exceedingly glad and grateful that I have learned this!" Ada has had opportunities to put the teachings into practice but she knows that she needs to be more fortified for the more challenging tests which lay on the long road ahead. However, due to the interplay between her dreams, changing circumstances, and emotional challenges, she is now more spiritually equipped and advanced in self-understanding than she has ever been!

Two Unusual Nurturing Experiences

As if all the above were not enough, Ada had the privilege of joining a group in Palenque in Chiapas, Mexico in December 2012. The intention was to celebrate through ceremonies at various sacred sites, the spiritual gifts of the Ancient Mayans whose formidable, sprawling temples still stand as immortal testimony to their cosmic presence and influence. After one of the ceremonies, Ada had an unusual experience of seeing above tall trees, what appeared to be three laughing fairies who blew shafts of light and love from their mouths straight towards her down below. It was as though this was a gift coming full circle from her first visit in Mexico over twenty years earlier! In Series Q, *Strange Figures,* a woman in Ada's dream gave her a gift, a blue heart shaped glass which she "put into a secret place." Ada became convinced that this was the concrete representation of the gift.

Following that 'encounter' with the fairies was the unforgettable walk in the nearby dark, cavernous labyrinth! During the walk, Ada realized the most frightening moment of fear she had ever known. She was at a point in such dense darkness, that she did not know where her next step would take her. Physically and psychologically, she was experiencing in that darkness, Braden's description of "the presence and nakedness," and "the abyss of nothing." It was a moment of sheer vulnerability, emptiness, non-attachment, and total surrender. In the darkness, she wondered what would happen if she made another step! Overcome with fear, she thought of crying out for help, then she recalled the guide's words at the entrance, "Don't think; just go with your feelings, trust your feelings." She slowly continued, step by step, eyes wide open, aware of nothing but the dark, with hands stretched forward as if she were blindfolded, and trusting the darkness. After moments which felt like eternity, gradually "feeling" her way alone through nowhere, a dim, distant glimmer of light became visible eventually leading to the exit. Ada realized she needed to be just by herself, still overcome by the extraordinary experience of the darkness as "hitting rock bottom" of her being. The feeling was a kind of brief recapitulation of the frustrating emotional emptiness which she had felt years earlier, only this time, there was a clarity, a suggestion of a baptism, a cleansing, a preparation and nourishment for the blooming. Later, while pondering this experience, Ada became aware of a rich level of significance in the meanings regarding two previous dreams.

Levels of Meaning

One dream relates to her Mom:

> *Mom is standing by an open door and she smilingly invites me to go in. The place is filled with light. We walk briefly together and then I am alone.*

An "open door," the invitation to enter, "filled with light," were dominant symbols in this predictive dream expressed much earlier in Ada's exploration. The open door was the opportunity to meet such teachers as Orloff and Braden, as well as experiences, such as Palenque. The darkness in that labyrinth provided moments of internal illumination. Encountering light as she walked through the open door represented the new insights and wisdom to be gained, all of which propelled Ada towards a triumphant feeling, a new perspective for healing her emotional self. She was then poised and freed for experiencing an awareness of her spiritual self which she had not yet known. She concluded that for good or for ill, at every moment, flowing within one's dynamic life process, one's emotional energy is linked with one's level of spiritual attainment. They simultaneously color one's interaction and response to self, others, and the vicissitudes of life.

Just before leaving New York, among dreams already mentioned, Ada had this dream:

> ## *I vividly see a two-tiered cake covered with white icing. With my forefinger, I dip into the icing, put some in my mouth and enjoy it!*

At first Ada interpreted "two tiered" to relate to two relocations before finally settling in her current environment, "the cake." The "icing" she believed, referred to the many interesting activities in which she became involved. She later realized that another level of meaning of her forefinger in the icing pertains to the following experience.

As if to bring to a climax the interesting series of spiritual adventures in 2012, Ada had an invaluable experience when she attended a lecture given by A.R.E's John Van Auken, a renowned scholar of the Edgar Cayce and Mayan teachings. Auken climaxed his informative lecture by a meditation which Ada found spellbinding. In essence, participants with closed eyes were directed to cleanse their thoughts through focused inhales and exhales, and concentrate on climbing, climbing as if on a ladder towards the heavens, as far and as high as possible. After attaining the highest possible point, all were to mentally repeat, "Rise my soul to Infinite Consciousness...rise my soul to Infinite Consciousness... rise my soul to Infinite Consciousness..." The visualization and the mantra were not only reminiscent of Ada's many climbing dreams; there was a feeling of rising along the most exhilarating climb of all!

By repeating the mantra, "Rise my soul to Infinite Consciousness" while visualizing climbing in meditation towards the heavens, Ada believed she understood another aspect of the *Why* of her dreams: *to daily, every moment, engage herself in the awareness of the authenticity of her true Self.* It was a feeling of dipping into and savoring the icing on the cake, relishing the sweetness of living the true, spiritual richness of the gift of life! By accepting this challenge, in every moment, she can privately experience her living indwelling divine nature of love, and like the begonia, consciously engage in enjoying her life as a continuous spiritual experience!

The second layer of the cake had yet another meaning. Out of curiosity, Ada attended another A.R.E. (Association for Research and Enlightenment) Conference in Virginia Beach where she was absolutely captivated by the demonstrations and healing effectiveness of past-life regression by Peter Woodbury, a master teacher of the Edgar Cayce teachings. Her long fascination with the relationship between reincarnation and current retarding or progressive life experiences of an individual was being played out right in front of her eyes! Her meeting with Sarah, the Canadian, represented by a bright star in Ada's dream, and who introduced her to reincarnation decades before, flashed vividly in her memory! This area of knowledge is now burgeoning as a field of healing and transformation! It was another layer of the cake, complete with the icing, in which, by her participation, Ada actively dipped her forefinger, and put it into her mouth by accepting, savoring and enjoying the stark truth and dynamic awakening of it all! These moments Ada will always recall with amazement!

CHAPTER TWENTY NINE

The spiritual journey is a movement towards freedom. Each stage liberates us from old patterns and gives us freedom to live the dream. Kaplan.[1]

Your dreams help you get in touch with your Higher Self, your True Self, the God part of you in such a way as to instill confidence in all the beauty, love, wisdom, power, and wonder that comprises the real you. Through dreams you can make that all-important God-connection. This is the real magic of dreams. Tanner [2]

ADDED ASSURANCE

After settling in her new home, Ada's first two dreams were ones where she was climbing again, predicting that she was in a place where she could experience new levels of spiritual enrichment.

I am ascending a staircase in a posh building of elegant architecture. Light is streaming through large windows of glass. It seems there is red carpet on the stairs and I am following a woman ahead of me but she is moving very quickly. I am finding it hard to keep up with her. I am led to the top of the stairs, I look around but she is nowhere in sight! (Ada awoke 4.46 a.m., and recorded this dream at 5:00 a.m. October 10, 2007, twelve days after occupying her new home. One month later, she had the following dream).

The mountain side is tall, bare, steep, almost vertical. I am climbing it and feeling the struggle of finding secure notches for my hand and feet. I am talking to God within and I am gradually being pulled up. Finally, my right fingers feel the sharp, secure, crusted edge at the top, and with unknown, unbelievable strength, I pull myself to the top, the pinnacle. I am not aware of a view, just a satisfying feeling of freedom and gratitude.

In the first dream, the quickly walking woman ahead of Ada appeared to be a spirit guide. The climbing dreams suggested that more elevating truths awaited her and she would be led to them as indicated by the light streaming through at the top of the stairs to which she was led.

Climbing, being pulled up, after much difficulty, and with "unbelievable strength" reaching the pinnacle in the second dream, seemed once again to indicate by her "feeling of freedom and gratitude," that Ada had reached a comfortable resolution to her long, arduous, inner archaeological quest. She felt free from the emotional entanglements she once experienced. She became independent of external standards, conformity to certain expectations, and outer forces of negativity which were formerly debilitating and retarding. She became free to engage with a higher level of empowering self-knowledge in an improved state of authentic joy and contentment. Ada felt a new spiritual identity for which she was seeking and to which she was subconsciously being led all along – the pinnacle of the mountain.

CHAPTER THIRTY

The dreams remind us that we are already what we have been striving to become, that we already have what we think we have been seeking... while it is necessary to go through all the stages of unfolding in order to fully know ourselves, our own divinity, we were there all along. Kaplan[1]

Self-knowledge is a most impressive oracle, crystallizing who you are and who you can be. As it mounts, expect to feel a coming together inside of you, a beautiful feeling of awakening. Orloff[2]

IN RETROSPECT

Ada's Mom introduced her to the dream world, then ushered her into the light through a doorway. Along her dream journey, she biked and drove uphill, entered elevators, flew in the air, encountered strange obstacles and negative vibrations, climbed rocks, stairs, hills, and mountains, delved deep to the ocean floor, heard music in various forms, and had visitations from children, known and unknown figures. Now in her retirement years, she took a challenging adventure into her innermost being to understand the *why* of such multiplicity of nightly enactments without her conscious direction! The exploratory experiences led her to realize that the mystery of every encounter, every seeming adversity, every emotional upheaval, every experience of joy, challenge, or unusual circumstance resulting from her choices, provided lessons to be learnt for soul growth. She was often blind, stubborn, and totally oblivious of the opportunities for learning, but Spirit never gave up on her. Self-knowledge was occurring in the total context of events, along many pathways and the perfection of circumstances. It often eluded her awareness, but in the process, she was destined to gradually identify, experience, and recognize her true being with freedom and gratitude, and aspire to harmonize with the Whole in this life. As Edgar Cayce explained, her dreams have truly been a "self-regulating, self-enhancing, self-training program" and Ada, the dreamer, in need of change, was at the center.

Her pre-sabbatical dream, ***While standing, I am looking at a badly shattered mirror***, reflected the imminent splintering of doubts of her personhood which were previously reinforced by layers of false conditionings of her real identity.

Assurance of an internal change was given in another later long predicted dream to which, except that it was positive, Ada was clueless to its meaning:

> *There is a light in my head and someone says, "This is your higher self." The light becomes a round object like a pearl and settles in the center of my left eye.* (SERIES N).

It was as if Ada was hearing the voice of Spirit,(her Higher Self) giving the light of illumination for her to see, to understand herself from a new perspective with wisdom represented by the pearl in her left eye.. In this context, the words of Breathnach acquires rich significance for Ada: "You and Spirit. The Dream team. The perfect couple. A match made in heaven to better the Earth...You fall in love for the first time and discover that your soul mate is Life."[3]

Earlier Abstraction Becomes Later Reality

Decades before, without understanding her own words, Ada had declared in the presence of a begonia, "that's how I should be...blooming**!**" From her recorded dreams, she studied the *what* and the *when* to find the *why* and what was missing . Now, in her retirement years, **ADA (A**ccess to **D**ivine **A**wakening), is being more spiritually aware, focused and nourished. The treasures of transformation found along the inner archaeological dig have been priceless. Emotional freedom as authentic spiritual consciousness is experientially being appreciated and incrementally being pursued within her as the clearing, climbing, and understanding continue. There is a new awareness of her self-worth rooted in recognition of Divine Essence within, a conviction that is being constantly revisited, confidently being fine-tuned and relished. With less frequency, illuminating dreams still occur and are given in-depth scrutiny for their messages....and ADA is ever mindful, ever grateful for their dynamic connection with all the events of her life with its many blessings... still occurring, magically expressing, but now with deep gratitude and reverence of its mysteries. She is now savoring moments of joy with a new freedom, with a new discovery of Self, the Essence of True Love, as an unchanging internal force, always available to Ada to experience her true self in egoless surrender. Now, there goes her current personal battle: the identifying, taming, and releasing of all ego attachments! Confirming the convictions of other spiritual luminaries, the wisdom of spiritual teacher, Eckhart Tolle captures the essence of self-knowledge even more succinctly in *The Power of Now:* "To know yourself as the Being underneath the thinker, the stillness underneath the mental noise, the love and joy underneath the pain, is freedom, salvation, enlightenment."[4] For Ada, this is "to feel a coming together inside of you," what it means to be truly alive, to be blooming!

While recognizing that the process of self-discovery through understanding is continuous, resulting from her long, inner journey of heroic digging and climbing reflected in her dreams, Ada now responds to Life from a new vista. Like a regenerating plant with flowering buds, expressions of joy, peace, freedom and gratitude color her moments and enrich her life. Like the begonia, she is being nourished by awareness of an inward abiding divine consciousness. She may continue to climb, but she can stop digging because all those dreams uniquely led her to the sacred, continuing awareness that the *why is in her expanding spiritual blooming*!

REFERENCES

Introduction
Chapter One: How it All Began

[1] Barrick., xiv-xv

[2] Kaplan,3

Chapter Two: A Recurring Dream and a Flower Speaks

[1] www.dreamtalk.htm,1-3, 2010.

[2] Breathnach, 165

Chapter Three: A Door Opens and a New Life Begins

[1] Sechrist, 233

Chapter Four: The Beginning of Profound Change

[1] Barrick., 55

[2] Craig Sim Webb. *Organic Dream Integration: Dream Interpretation and Meaning.* www.greatmystery.org. programs/article, 2013

[3] Barrick,28

Chapter Five: Emptiness Again Rears its Head

[1] Breathnach, 9,

[2] Praagh.,198

[3] Breathnach,155

Chapter Six: A Sabbatical Year And A Shift

[1] Breathnach,53

[2] Praagh,159

Chapter Seven: Answers From an Unexpected Source

[1] Kaplan, 42

[2] Orloff, 323

Chapter Eight: A Stranger to Herself

[1] Kaplan, 51

[2] Barrick, 67

[3]   Bro, 93

[4]   Praagh. 159.

Chapter Nine: Dreams Along Intertwining Pathways

[1]   Tanner,5

[2]   Barrick., 64

Chapter Ten: Teaching and Other Extra-Curricular Activities

[1]   Praagh, 198

[2]   Barrick, 203,

[3]   Bro.,145

[4]   Ibid, 149

[5]   Kaplan, 148-149

[6]   Breathnach,53

[7]   Sechrist., 26.

[8]   Bro,93.

Chapter Eleven: Selected Culminating Dreams and Symbols

[1]   Zukav, www.oprah.com/relationships/GaryZukav

[2]   Kaplan, 148

Chapter Twelve: An Illusion

[1]   Orloff,,374.

[2]   Barrick., 64

[3]   Orloff, 59, 2004

Chapter Thirteen: A New Shift in Self-Knowledge

[1]   Orloff,374

[2]   Furst, vii

Chapter Fourteen: Pathways to Experiences Beyond the Doorway

[1]   Guerrero, 22.

Chapter Fifteen: Endeavors, Hidden Treasures, and Dreams

[1]   Sechrist, 35

[2]   Barrick,56

[3]   Bro, 26

[4]   Orloff, 93

Chapter Sixteen: A Lecture and a Spotlight on the Emotions

[1] Zukav., 40-41

[2] Bennett-Goleman., 384

Chapter Seventeen: Emotional Freedom as Self-Knowledge

[1] Zukav., 40

[2] Kaplan., 141

[3] Orloff, 201

Chapter Eighteen: Dreams as a Career Ends as the Millennium Closes

[1] **Tanner, 6**

[2] Zukav, 159-160

Chapter Nineteen: A Blessed Experience

[1] Orloff, 50

[2] Bro, 114

Chapter Twenty: Interface of the Emotional and Spiritual Self

[1] Zukav, 39

[2] Bennett-Goleman, 179

[3] Orloff,374

Chapter Twenty One: Three Transformative Encounters

[1] Orloff, 323

[2] Smith, 211

[3] Orloff., 324

[4] Sechrist, 62

[5] Ibid, 61

[6] Breathnach, 124

Chapter Twenty Two: The Synchronicities: More Reflections and Lessons

[1] Zukav, 115

[2] Kaplan, 72

[3] Sechrist, 157

[4] Breathnach, 8

[5] Ferrini, 58

Chapter Twenty Three: Personalities, Transformation and Emotional Freedom

1.   Orloff, 374
2.   Singer, 106
3.   Frankl, 98
4.   Ibid, 108
5.   Breathnach, 165
6.   Frankl, 98
7.   Praagh, 198
8.   Breathnach, 41
9.   Kaplan, 155
10.   Orloff, 323
11.   Ibid, 323
12.   Kaplan, 157
13.   Tanner, 199, 2004

Chapter Twenty Four: Some Predictive Dreams and Messages

1.   Kaplan, 157
2.   Zukav, 160

Chapter Twenty Five: Changes, New Knowledge, and Dreams

1.   Barrck, 56,
2.   Orloff, 374

Chapter Twenty Six: Clues, Findings, Changes So Far Along the Journey

1.   Weiss, 177

Chapter Twenty Seven: Insights Leading To The Why

1.   Kaplan, 42
2.   Sechrist, 8

Chapter Twenty Eight: Nourishment for the Blooming

1.   Zukav, 67, 2010
2.   Weiss, 180.
3.   Braden, *DVD, 2007*

Chapter Twenty Nine: Added Assurance

1.   **Kaplan,** 246
2.   Tanner, 7

Chapter Thirty: In Retrospect - The Why Revealed

[1]   Kaplan, 229

[2]   Orloff, 59

[3]   Breathnach, 322

[4]   Tolle, 90

BIBLIOGRAPHY

Auken, John Van. *Personal Spirituality: The Presence.* Virginia Beach, VA: Association for Research and Enlightenment.

Auken, John Van. *How to Go From Karma to Grace.* Virginia Beach, VA: *A.R.E. Press,* 2011.

Barrick, Marilyn. *Dreams: Exploring the Secrets of Your Soul.* Corwin Springs, MT: Summit University Press, 1975

Bennett-Goleman, Tara. *Emotional Alchemy.* New York: Random House, 2001.

Braden, Gregg. *The Language of the Divine Matrix. DVD.* USA: Source Books, Inc.. 2007.

Breathnach, Sarah Ban. *Something More: Excavating Your Authentic Self.* New York: Time Warner Books, 1998.

Bro, Harmon. *Edgar Cayce on Dreams.* New York: Warner Books, Inc.,1968.

Browne, Sylvia. *Soul's Perfection.* Carlsbad, CA: Hay House, Inc., 2000.

Emoto, Masuru. *The True Power of Water.* Hillsboro, Oregon: Beyond Words Publishing, 2005

Ferrini, Paul. *Love Without Conditions: Reflections of the Christ Mind.* South Deerfield, MA: Heartways Press, 1994.

Frankl, V. *Man's Search For Meaning.* New York: Washington Square Press, 1954.

Furst, Jeffrey. *Edgar Cayce's Story of Attitudes and Emotions.* Toronto: Longmans Canada Ltd., 1972.

Heldman, Mary L. *When Words Hurt: How to Keep Criticism from Undermining Your Self-Esteem.* New York, Ballantine Books, 1988.

Kaplan, Connie. *Dreams are Letters from the Soul.* New York: Harmony Books, 2002.

Orloff, Judith, M.D. *Positive Energy.* New York: Harmony Books, 2004.

Orloff, Judith, M.D. *Emotional Freedom: Liberate Yourself From Negative Emotions and Transform Your Life.* New York: Harmony Books, 2009.

Praagh, James Van. *Unfinished Business: What the Dead Can Teach Us About Life. New York: Harper Collins, 2009.*

Sechrist, Elsie. *Dreams: Your Magic Mirror.* Virginia Beach, VA: A.R.E Press, 1995.

Sing, Tara. *Nothing Real Can be Threatened. Nothing Unreal Exists.* Los Angeles, CA: Life Action Press, 1989.

Singer, Michael. *The Untethered Soul.* Oakland, CA: New Harbinger Publications, Inc., 2007.

Smith, Dr. Robin L. *Hungry: The Truth About Being Full* . New York, Hay House, Inc., 2013.

Tanner, Wilda B. *Mystical Magical You.* Columbus, Ohio, Wild Comet Publishing, 2004.

Tanner, Wilda B. *The Mystical Magical Marvelous World of Dreams.* Columbus, Ohio: Wild Comet Publishing, 1988.

Taylor, Jeremy. *Where People Fly and Water Runs Uphill.* New York, Time Warner Books, 1992.

Thurston, Mark A., PhD. *How To Interpret Your Dreams.* Virginia Beach, VA: A.R.E. Press, 2007.

Tolle, Eckhart. *Practicing the Power of Now.* Novato, CA: New World Library, 2001.

Webb, Craig Sim. *Organic Dream Integration: Dream Integration and Meaning.. www.greatmystery.org/Programs/dreamsarticle. Sept. 20*, 2013.

Weiss, Brian, M.D. *Messages From the Masters*. New York: Grand Central Publishing, 2000.

Williamson, Marianne. *A Return To Love*. New York: Harper Collins, 1992.

Yogananda, Paramahansa. *Autobiography of a Yogi*. Los Angeles, CA: Self-Realization Fellowship, 1993.

Zukav, G. *How to Avoid Re-Creating Painful Situations. www.oprah.com/relationships/GaryZukav. Sept.21, 2012.*

Zukav, Gary. *Spiritual Partnership: The Journey to Authentic Power*. New York: Harper Collins Publishers, 2010.

Zukav, G. & Francis, L. *The Heart of the Soul: Emotional Awareness*. New York: Simon & Schuster, 2001.